THE
INVISIBLE
LINE

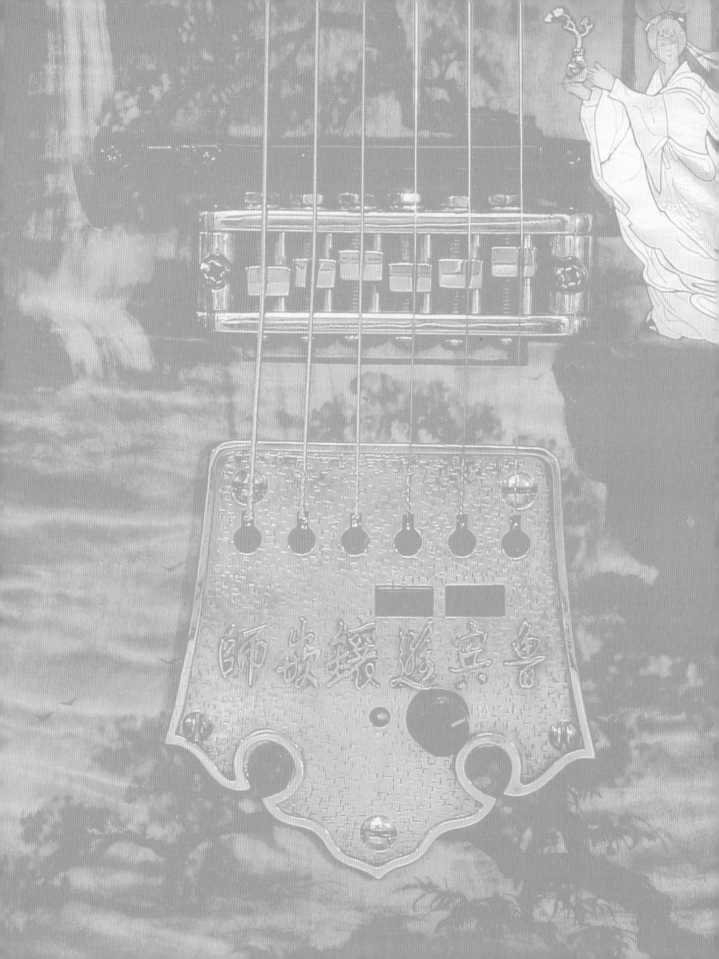

THE INVISIBLE LINE

When Craft Becomes Art

Edited by Larry Robinson

Hal Leonard Books
An Imprint of Hal Leonard LLC

Published in 2017 by Hal Leonard Books
An Imprint of Hal Leonard LLC
7777 West Bluemound Road
Milwaukee, WI 53213

Trade Book Division Editorial Offices
33 Plymouth St., Montclair, NJ 07042

Printed in the United States of America

Book design by Damien Castaneda

Library of Congress Cataloging-in-Publication Data
Names: Robinson, Larry, 1953–
Title: The invisible line : when craft becomes art / Larry Robinson.
Description: Milwaukee, WI : Hal Leonard Books, 2017.
Identifiers: LCCN 2016050406 | ISBN 9781617136535 (hardcover)
Subjects: LCSH: Guitar—Construction. | Guitar makers—United States.
Classification: LCC ML1015.G9 R57 2017 | DDC 787.87/1923—dc23
LC record available at https://lccn.loc.gov/2016050406

ISBN: 978-1-61713-653-5

www.halleonardbooks.com

To Connie,
who always has good ideas

❦

CONTENTS

FOREWORD BY TOM RIBBECKE ~ ix
INTRODUCTION BY LARRY ROBINSON ~ xi

1. DAVID GIULIETTI

2

2. BOB HERGERT

20

3. DAVID J. MARKS

38

4. MICHIHIRO MATSUDA

66

5. TOM RIBBECKE

84

6. LARRY ROBINSON

106

7. ERVIN SOMOGYI

134

AFTERWORD BY LARRY ROBINSON ~ 157
ACKNOWLEDGMENTS ~ 163
ABOUT THE ARTISTS ~ 165

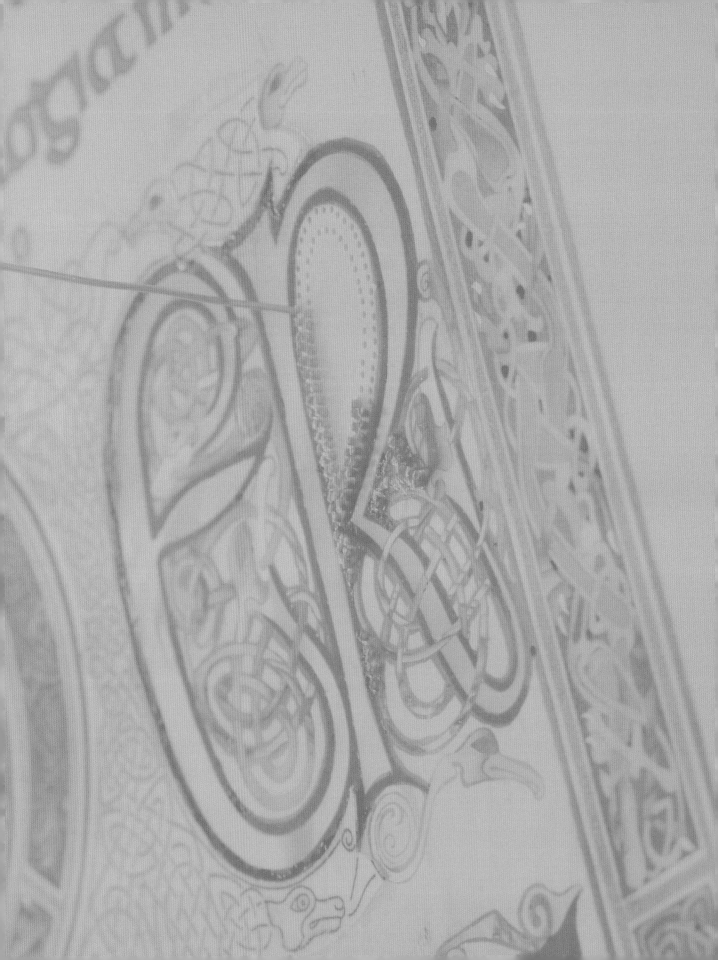

FOREWORD

From his humble shop in a woodsy, top-secret location in Northern California, Larry Robinson works diligently and consistently, surrounded by nature, bobcats, and tiny cutters whirring at many thousands of rpm. He is the maestro of the jeweler's saw, producing amazing and moving inlay work. Not just good, but considered to be the best by many, his work is very much like the man himself, disciplined and consistent.

Larry's body of work, created over more than four decades, proves that there is no one more facile at this wonderful visual art. Yet Larry has never been someone who makes lots of noise or seeks attention, even when we play music together (Larry is a fine bassist and we are band mates), but lets his magnificent work speak for itself. We have had many conversations about the topic of art and how we live with our compulsion to create. On many a rehearsal night I get to see his latest amazing inlay and it never ceases to impress me. I have had the privilege of collaborating with Larry many times, and my body of work is better for it.

This book brings together, at Larry's invitation, a collection of master artists and craftspeople of varied disciplines together totaling over three hundred years of collective pursuit of whatever it is we pursue! I am honored to write the foreword for a book that deals with the real "rubber meets the road" reality of a lifetime of creation and perspectives by some of the best in the world.

The reader who takes this opportunity to gain insight into each individual artist and story may never look at art the same way again. I expect the book will be helpful in figuring out where that "invisible line" really is and will deepen the understanding of why we all do what we do. Enjoy the journey!

—Tom Ribbecke

INTRODUCTION

Not long after *The Art of Inlay* was published, my wife, Connie, said to me, "In your next book, there should be a section detailing the difference between art and craft, since you're always hearing from people who want to tell you that everything you do is a major work of art." We both know that wasn't true, since a good portion of my daily bread is made by inlaying exactly what customers ask me to inlay, whether it's a signature or flowers or an image of their deceased pet on a peghead. I always try to work as if each inlay will be the last one I ever do and that's what my entire career will be judged upon, so the craft level stays consistent throughout, but there is definitely a difference between these projects and ones in which I'm allowed to express myself more freely.

Once that idea was rolling around in my brain, the realization set in that people have attempted to define these parameters since humans could speak, and that the definitions in dictionaries are only helpful to a point, because everybody has their own opinion, and, regardless of what the educated art historians and critics would have you believe, your opinion is as good as anyone's. That's when I decided to enlist some help.

The collaborators in this book are all friends of mine. They have a variety of backgrounds, and at least one has an art degree. Most, but not all, are either luthiers or immersed in the guitar-building milieu. Those who are not have at least done some fantastic artwork on custom-made instruments, and you will see their other creative passions as well. I asked them to write their thoughts about what constituted a piece of art as opposed to craft, and put no limits on word count or anything else, for that matter. Nobody got to see what the other contributors wrote (except for me, of course, but mine was already done). The differences and similarities in each section make for an interesting conversation. The photos tell their own story.

And for that, we have to thank the sun. Aside from the fact that without it we wouldn't be here, the photons it sends our way at 186,000 miles per second allow us to discriminate between objects as they bounce off them. When full-spectrum light hits an object, many of the wavelengths are absorbed, and what is left is reflected, some to the cones in your eyes, which translate the leftover spectra as color after a bit of hocus-pocus in the brain. This is a subjective process, partly due to physical differences in each individual's eye structure, which means that people can see the same color differently. Once you overlay environmental and genetic filters, it's amazing that we can agree on anything. So it's not surprising to me that people have come up to me at guitar shows and pointed to my China guitar, saying, "That's art!" and in the same breath looked at the "Meet the Beetles" guitar and said, "That's not!" Ten minutes later someone would come by and say the opposite.

So enjoy your foray into the high weeds, and try not to throw anything when the discussion becomes animated. And, while you're at it, go make some art.

THE
INVISIBLE
LINE

FIGURE 1.1. **Aqua quadrille ring. Sterling silver, 18k yellow gold and Santa Maria aquamarine.** Photo by Hap Sakwa

1

DAVID GIULIETTI

He who works with his hands is a laborer.

He who works with his hands and his head is a craftsman.

He who works with his hands and his head and his heart is an artist.

—ST. FRANCIS OF ASSISI

Merriam-Webster defines "craft" as "an activity that involves making something in a skillful way by using your hands" or "a job or activity that requires special skill." Craft disciplines came out of a history of passing on ways of making from one generation to the next. Historically, this has been an important part of how human technology has advanced. The craft workshop has been a way of preserving and transmitting existing knowledge and has

---

FIGURE 1.2. **Blue Lunar Cluster ring. Palladium, sapphire, diamonds.** I made this ring because I wanted to play with some ideas for achieving a sophisticated-looking piece using very simple techniques layered together. What you can't see in the photo is a beautiful tulip rosette pierced out behind the stone inside of the ring. This was my first fabricated ring in palladium, and it drove me crazy at first because the torch kept turning the palladium bright blue. Everything I had read said you could get rid of the blue color using the torch, but I wasn't able to do it. Luckily it polished up quite nicely anyway. Photo by Hap Sakwa

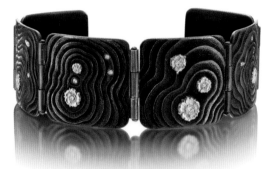

FIGURE 1.3. **Cathedral band. 18k yellow gold with rose-cut diamonds.** The engraving on this ring is based on a cathedral floor plan by Filippo Brunelleschi, one of the foremost architects of the Italian Renaissance. Doing the engraving was fairly easy, but the layout was difficult. Everything had to be just perfect for the design to line up and work. Photo by Hap Sakwa

FIGURE 1.4. **Cherry Blossom panel bracelet. Sterling silver, 18k gold and diamonds.** This bracelet took weeks to make. I built the clasp from a plan in a book on clasps and hinges. I followed the plan exactly, but when I finished the clasp didn't work at all. It took some seat-of-the-pants engineering to redesign it after it was already all soldered in place. Luckily, I was able to make it work quite nicely with a modified gateleg design. What I remember most about this bracelet was the many hours of punchwork in the engraved water pattern. My wrist was sore for days after this was finally done. Photo by Hap Sakwa

been fundamental in creating the foundation for innovation in the working of materials.

You only need to pick up a tool for a few hours to begin to appreciate the millennia of collected knowledge that makes the most basic manipulation of materials possible. When I lift a torch in my studio and solder a gold bezel, there are generations of careful study and experimentation that have made that thirty-second operation possible. The torch itself is a highly evolved means of controlling the same fire our caveman ancestors used to roast wild animals. The valves in the handpiece that allow me to control the flame represent centuries of collective information in mining, metallurgy, chemistry, casting, and machining. The propane gas that burns, the purified oxygen that causes the flame to burn hotter, the borax

FIGURE 1.5. **Cherry Blossom signet ring. Sterling silver, 18k gold and diamonds.** After being inspired by the sword furniture of Tokugawa-period Japan, I had been doing some gold inlay in silver pieces, which were beautiful but time-consuming to build. I decided to experiment with a solder overlay technique on this. The ring was finished the night before my first juried craft show. You never really know what a piece like this is going to look like as you work on it, because the black patina is the last element to go on the ring. It was a glorious sight when it came out of the patina solution at one thirty in the morning. Photo by Hap Sakwa

FIGURE 1.6. **Chrysanthemum cuff. Sterling silver, 18k and 22k gold, aquamarine, labradorite, diamonds.** I misread my flight information leaving the American Craft Council show in Baltimore and ended up at the airport four hours early. The airport turned out to be a wonderful place for me to work on drawings. I was able to draw this bracelet in its entirety along with the design for my Moon Curve earrings. When I got back to the studio I tried to rework the drawing, which would be what I would normally do with a sketch, but I found that I couldn't alter a single line without hurting the composition. Now I am always eager to get an hour or two at the airport to draw: no phones, no computer, and nobody knocking on the door. Photo by Hap Sakwa

flux that prevents the joint from oxidizing, the carefully alloyed gold solder, and even the red sable paintbrush used to position tiny bits of solder on the joint, are possible because of thousands of years of preservation and innovation in strategies of making.

One of the more interesting aspects of working in a craft discipline is the constant back-and-forth dynamic between the individual and the group. Even though the techniques used have passed through thousands of hands over time, it is the individual craftsperson that learns the techniques and puts them to use breathing life and form into silk, steel, plastic, and wood. Although it is possible for legions of craftspersons to essentially make the same object the same way for many lifetimes, it only takes one cockeyed person to

FIGURE 1.7. **Coral briolettes. 18k gold, rose-cut diamonds and red coral.** The color of red coral paired with yellow gold strikes a chord in me. I feel this combination all the way down into my Italian roots. The beautiful thing about these is that they are all hand fabricated, so they are as light as a feather. Photo by Hap Sakwa

FIGURE 1.8. **Gun Scroll pendant. Sterling silver, 18k gold, pink sapphire, tourmaline, diamonds.** This pendant came out of the same batch of work as the Edward ruby ring. Working simply and directly on the metal, I would rub wax on the metal and then draw the design into it with a pencil. The resulting firearms scroll feels flowing and alive. Photo by Hap Sakwa

turn the whole thing on its head by simply looking at something in a new way. This is sort of interesting, because it points to an important function of the craft discipline. Craft can function, not just as a database and transmitter of collected information, but as an airstrip or receiver for the individual craftsperson to land a new idea. Craft as a day-to-day studio practice is a simple and direct way to take an inspired moment and fully realize the possibility contained therein. All the brilliant ideas in the world are meaningless if they find no way to transition from misty apparition into some sort of earthly format.

So, if craft is a collector, transmitter, and receiver of information, when does it become art?

FIGURE 1.9. **Edward ruby ring. Ruby cabochon, sterling silver, 18k gold and diamond.** A critique group I was in prompted this ring design. Russ Larman had been encouraging me to really push to exploit the use of engraving in my work. I had been wanting to experiment with asymmetrical designs drawn freehand on the metal without a preliminary sketch. This ring was part of the first wave of that method of working. Photo by Hap Sakwa

FIGURE 1.10. **Inlaid steel band. Steel, 18k rose gold, 22k yellow gold.** With a little help from Larry Robinson, this ring was machined out of a steel nut from the hardware store. I had been doing some gold inlay in stainless steel on some of Dan Burke's folding knives and I wanted to experiment with a ring. The 22k yellow gold was a breeze to inlay, but the rose gold gave me fits. It would work-harden while I was hammering it into the cavity so that by the time I got from one end of the little piece of gold to the other it would pop itself out. I spent the better part of a weekend on my knees looking for the little gold chunks on the floor. Photo by Hap Sakwa

Merriam-Webster defines art as "something that is created with imagination and skill that is beautiful or that expresses important ideas or feelings." A working definition of art is elusive by nature. Identifying a work of art is a subjective process that depends less upon the quality of the work than it does upon the abilities of the audience. Lacking a knowledgeable and receptive audience, a maker may be able to imbue a project with the depth, mystery, and beauty we associate with great creative works but still live unrecognized, lost in the shuffle. Regardless of a piece's intrinsic merit, the power to acknowledge a work of art lies with the critical public. Working in this environment can be fairly challenging, and it is no wonder that artists have gained a reputation in our

FIGURE 1.11. **Moon Curve earrings. Sterling silver, 18k gold, 22k gold, moonstone, diamonds.** These earrings came out of a conversation with Tom Herman. Tom, who is an excellent saw piercer, liked my engraving quite a bit but pointed out that with a little saw work I could get much more drama with less effort. I decided to take his advice to heart. Photo by Hap Sakwa

FIGURE 1.12. **Oculus pendant. 18k gold and rose-cut diamonds.** The pendant was part of a group, along with the Oculus ring. The oculus, or "eye of heaven," was the small window in the top of cathedral domes. Photo by Autumn Swisher

society for occasionally being eccentric and difficult to deal with.

This triangle between artist, art object, and viewer may have quite a bit to do with why the myth of Prometheus is so often associated with artistic creation. In the psychological inner world of the artisan, those with the power to grant validity to one's most intimate output take on a god-like authority. The feeling of crawling in the mud, waiting for the gods to give the nod to your existence, tends to create a situation in which the opinions of the authorities must be blocked out, pushed aside, or otherwise dodged so that the creative act can occur. Like Prometheus, the artist is forced to steal fire from the gods by seizing the power to identify his or her own work as valid. This issue is

FIGURE 1.13. **Padparadscha ring. 18k gold, padparadscha sapphire and tourmalines.** My client for this ring wanted a lotus flower–themed ring. I came up with the idea for using the lotus leaves to form the setting for the center stone. It was an experimental setting, and padparadscha stones are quite pricey, so I ended up spending almost an entire week, with sweaty hands, just setting the center stone. I would go in and shave metal off the inside of the setting and then stare at it, trying to figure out what would be the perfect position to make the setting work. In the end the stone went down perfectly. Photo by Hap Sakwa

FIGURE 1.14. **Oculus ring. 18k gold and rose-cut diamonds.** The oculus design comes out of my love of Renaissance cathedral architecture. I had been looking at a lot of pictures of antique diamond cluster rings and I wanted to do my own version. This one has a pierced tulip rosette on the curved plate behind the stones that rests on the finger. Photo by Hap Sakwa

complicated even more by the fact that genuine perceptive ability is rare. A critic with the integrity and aesthetic capacity to recognize an unknown work of art is in a very small club. Most critics, much like the majority of artists, are not contributing original thought to the discussion but are mainly doing the everyday work of building out the language around the already recognized and approved channels of artistic knowledge.

The relationship between artist, artwork, and audience is very important. It is essential to an artist's output to receive recognition as a creator of legitimate works of art in the eyes of the critical public. Beyond the legitimization of the maker's efforts, and any tangible benefits in the form of money or notoriety, this relationship can also be useful to

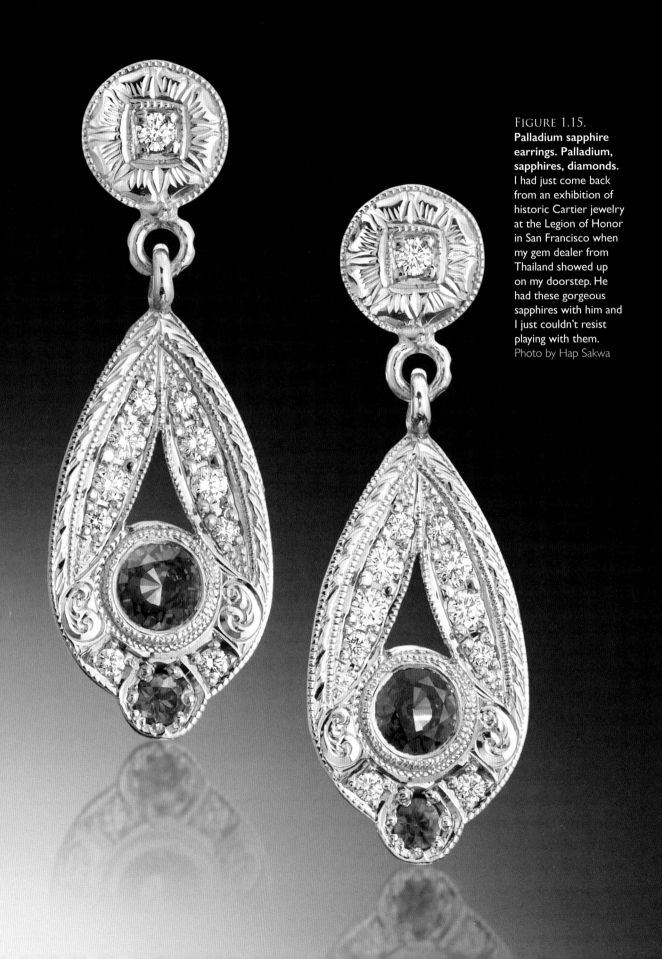

FIGURE 1.15.
Palladium sapphire earrings. Palladium, sapphires, diamonds.
I had just come back from an exhibition of historic Cartier jewelry at the Legion of Honor in San Francisco when my gem dealer from Thailand showed up on my doorstep. He had these gorgeous sapphires with him and I just couldn't resist playing with them.
Photo by Hap Sakwa

FIGURE 1.16. **Pierced chalcedony. Sterling silver, 18k gold, chalcedony, orange sapphire.** The arms that form the bail on this pendant/necklace are hand-forged out of thick pieces of silver. They are then filed, engraved, and attached with solder to flow perfectly into the main body of the piece. Photo by Hap Sakwa

the creative process itself. The back-and-forth dialogue between artist and viewer can help artists to understand their own work and to align and orient their internal creative direction. Often, artists are much better at creating their art than they are at explaining their work, and it is the critics who help develop the language necessary to communicate the meaning to the world. Pablo Picasso spent a great deal of time talking to his friends who were critics and art experts, and their input gave him a greater ability to talk about and understand the impact of his own work. If you are going to steal fire from the gods, it can be useful to make friends with them first. That way you know where they hide the spare key.

Beyond the artist–audience relationship, what is it about a creative work that gives

FIGURE 1.17. **Purple sapphire cabochon ring.** Sterling silver, 14k and 18k gold, sapphire cabochon and rose-cut diamonds. I had wanted to make a gold ring with a lot of surface for engraving, and I had this beautiful purple sapphire. The asymmetrical engraving, off-center main stone, and rich color give the ring a wonderful visual energy. Photo by Hap Sakwa

**FIGURE 1.18.
Sapphire Orbit
pendant. Steel, 22k
and 18k gold, sapphire.**
This was another piece
using gold inlay in steel
with all the other gold
elements riveted onto
the work. I wanted to
keep the design clean
and minimal with just
a tiny bit of hammer
texture on the bail and
setting. I figured out that
a well-used cup bur with
a little polishing makes
an excellent miniature
riveting anvil. Photo by
Hap Sakwa

FIGURE 1.19. **Rose-cut garnet pendant. Sterling silver, 18k gold, diamonds.** The idea for this pendant popped into my head while I was in the shower. I went into the studio and worked on it for three solid days. I showed it to Shaya, my studio partner, when it was done, and she said, "Nice! I wondered what you were working on so intensely for the last few days." Photo by Hap Sakwa

it intrinsic aesthetic value and makes it art? What elevates a well-crafted object to the realm of art? Marcel Duchamp would say that the artist, in simply declaring something to be a work of art, makes it so. There are very specific conditions which make this possible, and it can be a little more difficult to exhibit a store-bought urinal and call it art in the world of craft than in the world of fine art. So what is it that makes a ceramic vessel stop being an ordinary pot and begin to vibrate with the resonant beauty we associate with art? What does the individual artist bring to the table that allows him or her to transcend being a constructor of physical objects and become the spirit that informs the process?

In my own production as a maker, and in the works of many other craftsman

FIGURE 1.20. **Scroll trillion earrings. 18k gold, citrine and diamonds.** I learned while making these that trillion-cut stones have a way of making almost any design look modern, and really had to play with these to get them to feel a little more like my style. I was rushing a little while setting the second citrine and cracked it. Luckily, I was able to get an exact match from my Brazilian gem dealer, and after a little careful annealing of the gold the earrings were saved. Photo by Hap Sakwa

FIGURE 1.21. **Coral quadrille earrings. Red coral, sterling silver, 18k gold.** Spanish western spur engraving inspired this design. The red coral, black silver, and yellow gold have such a rich elemental feel to them. I am always amazed at what a little engraving does to a simple silver disc. Photo by Hap Sakwa

and artists, I have noted pieces that have an elusive quality about them that is difficult to define. When I look back at my own production, there are specific objects that seem to have an indefinable strength to them. It is rarely something I plan to do. They seem to be a product of circumstances beyond my control. There is no apparent connection to my level of ability or where they occur in the timeline of creative output. They come through often by dumb luck. These pieces are charged with something. I can look at a piece after not seeing it for fifteen years and it still rings with energy. It isn't something I can force. I am not sure if we can set out to make a piece of art. That would be like waking up in the morning and deciding that today I am going to make a new friend who will become my best friend ever. The best I can do is to create conditions where there is a possibility that if some interesting idea comes down the pike I am standing ready with a net to try and catch it. Some people will cringe at this antique idea of the magical aura of the precious objet d'art, but it is what gets me excited to get out of bed in the morning and head to the bench.

I have known with a fair amount of certainty since high school that I would be some sort of artist. It was clear to me that my temperament and abilities suited me well for the role and at the same time made me a bad fit for most other occupations (special end of the sandbox). I studied fine art in college, and at the time of graduation I was producing conceptual, postmodern work. I could think, create, write, and speak like a contemporary fine artist, but I had almost no knowledge at all of the world of craft.

After a six-month post-graduation road trip, I ended up broke and in need of employment on the central coast of California. There was a local art bronze foundry that was hiring metal finishers. I had taken a foundry class in school and learned some of the basics of how to create a model in wax and cast it in bronze, though I had abandoned all my school pieces at the rough casting stage. There was very little instruction in finishing, and I think deep down I had a notion that all the sanding, polishing, and cleanup involved was somehow beneath me as a gifted "artiste." All that aside, I was pretty good with my hands and thought I pretty much knew it all. I applied at the foundry and thought they would jump at the chance to hire a recently graduated art student with an entire semester of foundry experience under my belt. I had to call every day, twice a day, for two weeks before they realized they had better hire me just to get me to stop bugging them. After only a few hours on the job the supervisor realized how much I knew about properly chasing and finishing bronze . . . absolutely nothing.

What I saw right away was that most of the workers were strictly skilled trade labor. They could do the technical work, but they didn't have the artistic skills and training to design or create original pieces. For the most part they didn't have the ability to analyze a piece and verbalize what it was about it that made it good or bad. They also tended to think that anatomical correctness seemed to be what made a piece good. This made for some interesting confusion when they were confronted with pieces that were appealing on an emotional level but didn't exhibit any technical virtuosity or advanced knowledge of anatomy.

Clearly, there is a dividing line where the craftsman's work begins to take on more visually advanced features, which we associate with works of art. Those features might include, but not be limited to, shapes or proportions that reference earlier works of art or nature, or color pairings that suggest a different shade, and the general utilization of materials and form to bring forth a certain mood or feeling. It may seem like the ability to design makes one an artist, but our tendency as a culture to view intellectual white-collar activities as superior to blue-collar labor tends to bias our judgment a little. It can seem at first glance that it is the intellectual ability to design that can make an object into art, but design in and of itself is not art. Parking lots, toilet plungers, and ketchup bottles are all designed by someone and are rarely referred to as great works of art. We have all experienced music, film, writing, and other art works that are skillfully made, thoughtfully designed, but are dull and spiritless.

Craft starts to transition into the more ephemeral world of art when certain conditions are in place. The maker is searching for a way to skillfully manipulate materials together with a meaningful design. Sometimes the design is preplanned, or else it is roughly laid out with the specifics being discovered as the piece progresses. When the craftsperson has enough of a grasp of the material process coupled with a good understanding of design, an element of internal elegance can begin to surface within the piece. This elegance can be like a balloon or a sail that fills up to the degree of the artist's ability and courage to follow where it leads.

Personal qualities of the artist become woven into the piece. If craft itself is a vehicle for collecting and transmitting strategies of making, then we can think about the art part of it as a series of strategies for the transfer of complex information. When artists work, they bring their own individual history and frame of reference to the process. These

FIGURE 1.22. **C. F. Martin millionth guitar.** This is the back of guitar manufacturer C. F. Martin's serial number 1,000,000 guitar. Larry Robinson spent over two years working on this guitar, and he hired me to do some engraving on a few bits. I carved the acanthus ornament on the sides of the bridge out of 18k gold sheet.

The gold rosette at the center of the soundhole was fashioned out of a piece of sheet gold using a graver, a saw, and a few files. These parts, along with engraving the braces on the inlay of a guitar top on the pickguard, took about a week and a half. I spent another five weeks doing the faces of the angels and the portrait of C. F. Martin, Sr. on the back. I got these parts to work on after Larry had already put two years into them. No pressure. Photo by Larry Robinson

are complex structures comprised of personal, political, formal, emotional, or intellectual information—all of their life experience. This is why they talk about head, hands, and heart in the making of a piece of art. If the artist intentionally or by accident goes deeply inside himself or herself, it can be reflected in the material. When this is done with a subtle hand, the work can touch a deeper chord. It is this profound, even universal element that a viewer can feel when experiencing the piece. This is why people talk about the aura surrounding great works of art. It is often referred to as truth or beauty, because it is a simple way of stating something that eludes words. Experiencing a work of art can be transformative, perhaps even more so if it appears from your own hand.

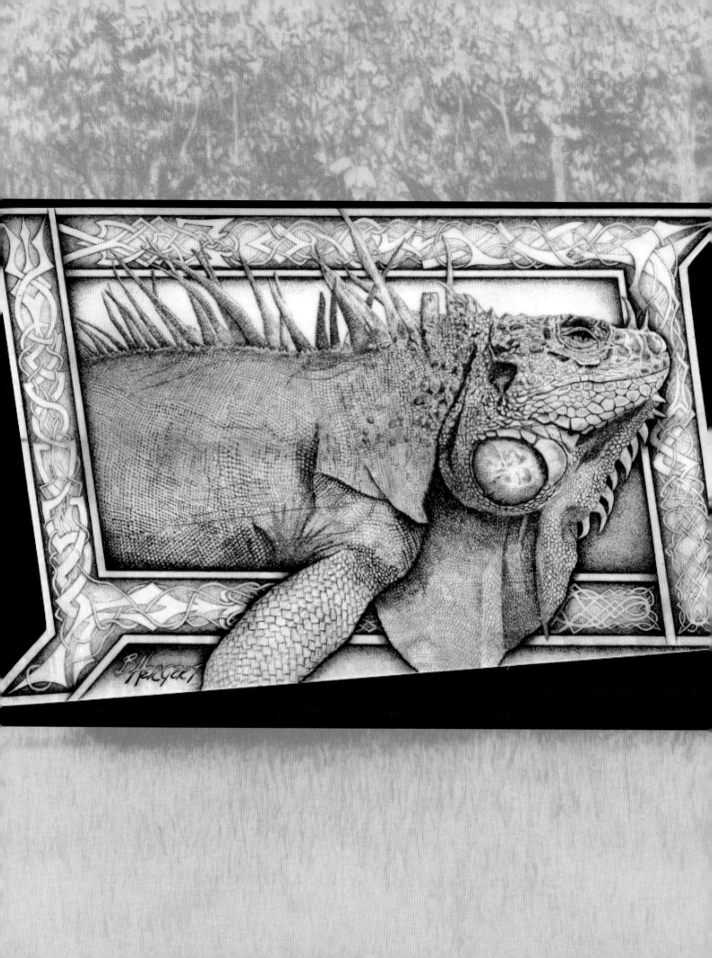

2
BOB HERGERT

One summer day I stood in the backyard underneath the willow tree. I was in a thoughtful mood, pondering the mysteries of life. OK, let's just say my mind was wandering. For me, one of the biggest mysteries was, "What is art?" I was trying to come up with a definition of art. At this period in my life, I was struggling in my mind, wondering if I could presume to call myself an artist. I felt if my work fit the description of art then surely I could call myself an artist—and back it up. For a while I felt like this was my search for the lost chord or El Dorado. Then it came to me. Yes! Finally I had it, succinct and complete. I really should have grabbed a pen, because I got busy doing something else and I completely forgot that profound combination of words!

To this day I've never been able to remember what that "inspired" definition was. Maybe that's some kind of metaphor for art itself. We think we can put words or limits on something that is impossible to contain with words. Should we even try? With so

---

FIGURE 2.1. **Iguana.** I describe this as my favorite piece of scrimshaw. My goal was to suggest this iguana breaking out of its two-dimensional bounds. When I see great pieces of art, especially scrimshaw, I think, "I wish I had done that." When I see this, I think, "Did I really do that?" (3" x 5"). Photo by Bob Hergert

FIGURE 2.2. **Carson.** This small portrait is on a guitar truss rod cover. In many ways a simple portrait is the most satisfying subject, and the most difficult. As I work on a portrait I feel a humbling connection with the Creator. To see eyes come to life and look back at you is a feeling like no other. (1.7" x 2.2"). Photo by Bob Hergert

many books titled "The Art of (fill in the blank)," it might be possible to believe that everything is art, but for my purposes, I'll stick to what are generally considered "fine arts"—painting, sculpture, architecture, music, and poetry. Within the painting category I include other two-dimensional work like drawing, printmaking, and scrimshaw.

Late one night I was looking at a piece of scrimshaw I had done a few years before. I hadn't studied it since I had finished it. I got caught up in the details and the subtleties of the piece, and for a while I felt as if someone else had created it. I had become just an observer and felt no ownership or pride. Without my ego involved, I was able to enjoy it in a way I never had. It now became easier for me to feel it was inspired.

FIGURE 2.3. **Claire Martin.** Claire Martin, daughter of C. F. Martin IV, on a miniature Martin Guitar headstock. I made this as a gift to Chris Martin to thank him for letting me work on Martin's 1.5 millionth guitar. So, if nothing else of mine gathers dust in the back room of some museum, at least the Martin guitar will be around long after I am not. (1.5" x 3"). Photo by Bob Hergert

I grew up drawing pictures. Every childhood birthday and Christmas meant gifts of crayons, paints, coloring books, or modeling clay. I didn't know and certainly didn't care that I was building a set of skills that would become second nature. As a child with a vivid imagination, I could daydream not only in my mind, but on paper, too. I was off and running. I had found

FIGURE 2.4. **Cossacks.** A scene based on two paintings by the Ukrainian painter Repin. Complicated scenes with lots of characters keep work interesting. (3" x 5"). Photo by Bob Hergert

something I liked to do and I was good at it.

I'm not sure why it should matter, but I struggled with the concept of calling myself an artist. For some reason, either from ignorance or timidity, I hesitated to call drawing "art." To me, painting and sculpture were the epitome and drawing the preparation. This may have been the classic example of "a little learning is a dangerous thing." I would visit galleries and museums and see the prominence of painting and the general lack of drawings. It wasn't until years later that an art historian I met figuratively knocked some sense into me. He made it perfectly clear that drawing is the foundation of the graphic arts. So at least one problem was solved. I realized finally that drawing is art.

FIGURE 2.5. **Cossacks detail.** Close-up showing the detail of the client's son's name written in Cyrillic script. It's fun to throw in these "hidden" bits that reward anyone who looks closely enough to find them. Photo by Bob Hergert

These days I admit I have no definition for art that can serve as a filter or a scale. But every time I do a piece of work I look at it when I'm finished and wonder if it is art. Certainly not every piece is, but some are. I'd like to think that my work that doesn't rise to the level of art is instead fine craft. So, what factors take a piece from craft to art? One is originality. With some disciplines originality is easier to achieve. Painting, certainly, with its nearly unlimited palette, is one. And then there are music and poetry. I'll have more to say about those in a bit.

Traditional scrimshaw is the art of incising, or cutting, into the surface of ivory or bone to produce images. Most scrimshaw is done on fossil ivory and ivory substitutes. The cuts

FIGURE 2.6. **Davey.** Guitarist and poet
H. Home (David Sevedge). I was especially
proud of being able to maintain the scale
of the guitar strings—and to capture the
joy in the face of this phenomenal guitarist.
(3.5" x 4.5"). Photo by Bob Hergert

FIGURE 2.7. **Dragon pen.** "Dancing dragons" and modified Celtic knots grace this ivory and gold fountain pen.
Photo by Bob Hergert

made in the polished surface are filled with pigment, usually paint or ink. The pigment is then wiped from the smooth surface. The cuts in the ivory become the image. My scrimshaw is lines and dots. Essentially, it's drawing with a scribe, which is a metal bar with a fine, pointed tip, much like engraving. There's no erasing, no reworking or painting over mistakes.

Let's compare the art of scrimshaw to music. The scrimshaw artist has a small palette to work with. Musicians have twelve notes and thousands of instruments to work with. Most musical compositions are recognizable after just a few notes. Uniqueness in music is almost unavoidable. Among other things, music is distinguished by rhythm and dynamics. With scrimshaw the rhythm and dynamics, that is, the flow and softness or

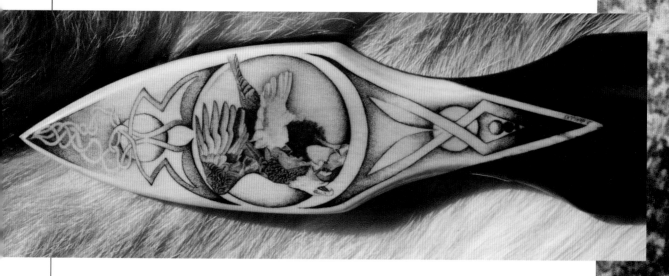

FIGURE 2.8. Eagle letter opener. A swooping eagle framed by some free-form design. I've done countless wildlife images, so sometimes I step out a bit (or should I say "go overboard"?) with embellishments. (2.5" x 1.25"). Photo by Bob Hergert

FIGURE 2.9. End of the Trail. Before I began doing scrimshaw, most of my drawings were pen-and-ink and pencil. I did this with black and gray crayon pencils. I used to drive by this relic on the way to the Oregon coast from Portland. I knew it wouldn't last forever, but I hoped my drawing would. (18" x 24"). Photo by Bob Hergert

hardness of impact, are in the execution but not necessarily evident in the final product. Or we can contrast drawing and poetry. Poets have thousands of words to use. And so a single phrase or rhyme can bring to mind the author. With rare exceptions, drawings need a lot of detail to achieve uniqueness. My point here is to show how difficult it is to be original with drawing. It's not difficult to see the difference between the paintings of say, Raphael and Michelangelo, but it can be tough to tell the differences between drawings by each.

However, originality is only a part of art, and certainly a small part

FIGURE 2.10.
Guitar knob. One of two ivory knobs on my Galletta electric guitar. I do a lot of work on guitars I don't get to play, so I make sure all of mine have something **personal, too.** Photo by Bob Hergert

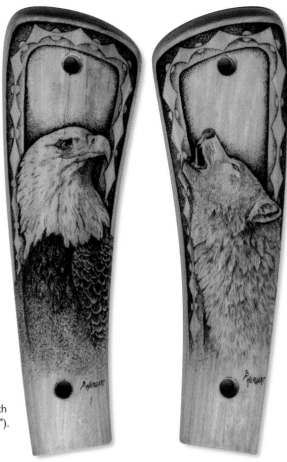

FIGURE 2.11. **Knife handles.** A pair of knife scales on Russian woolly mammoth ivory. Wildlife, with just that extra touch. (1" x 3").
Photo by Bob Hergert

of subject matter. Some of the greatest Western art depicts nothing more spectacular than a face or a figure, a harbor, or haystacks in a field. The more mundane the subject, the more important becomes the execution. I have to remind myself not to agonize over subject matter, but instead to make the simplest thing sublime. Maybe this is part of what separates craft from art. Craft needs to serve a purpose, but it doesn't necessarily have to inspire or create a sense of wonder. Craft can satisfy its purpose and please the viewer or user. It doesn't need to do more. Great craft reflects what is best of human effort—training, practice, experience, and execution. Great art reflects something that's more than human effort, and that is inspiration.

FIGURE 2.12. **Mary D. Hume.** Fossil walrus artifact with a memorial scene. This boat will soon be at the bottom of the Rogue River on the southern Oregon coast. The ten-thousand-year-old ivory seemed a perfect medium. The natural coloring of the ivory seemed to suggest fog, consistent with the scene's actual environment. (2" x 6"). Photo by Bob Hergert

FIGURE 2.13. **Morgan Peso.** I've collected interesting bills and coins for years. So, just for fun, I tried my hand at "counterfeiting." I inlaid the ivory bill into a walnut box top. There was no way I intended to duplicate each line of the engraved bill, so this was a wonderful lesson in translation from line to stippled dots. The coin is actual size, the bill slightly smaller than actual size. (2" x 5"). Photo by Bob Hergert

Another element common to art is style. Style to me is like a habit that can't be broken, and one we don't want to break. Where some people find themselves unconsciously tapping their foot to music I've always found myself sketching, doodling. I vividly remember back as a freshman in high school sitting in class, apparently paying no attention to the teacher as I drew pictures on my notepad. The teacher made some important point and then as a surprise, without looking at me, asked, "Hergert, what did I just say?" I was able to repeat it verbatim. I think he gave me a slight smile, and after that he never bothered me about my drawing in class. I mention this because this semiconscious drawing seemed to come through without filters. And so, too, this habit of drawing began to reveal my style. I have

FIGURE 2.14. **Old Ghost Highway.** Capturing scenes that will soon be lost to the march of time has always intrigued me. This collection of cars was on the Coast Highway near my home. (2" x 3"). Photo by Bob Hergert

FIGURE 2.15. **One Line.**
When I was in my late teens
I discovered technical pens.
The ability to control line
width made it possible for me
to create this drawing in one
continuous line. (8" × 10"). Photo
by Bob Hergert

FIGURE 2.16. **Waterloo
Tooth.** If someone
knows nothing else about
scrimshaw they might at
least associate it with the
whalers' art of incising
sperm whale teeth. This
large tooth is an homage
to the early days of the
art. The ship is the *HMS
Waterloo*. Getting everything
right in a nautical scene
like this is important to me
and takes a lot of time. The
rigging, the sails, the lines,
and even the surface of the
water need to be "real."
Photo by Bob Hergert

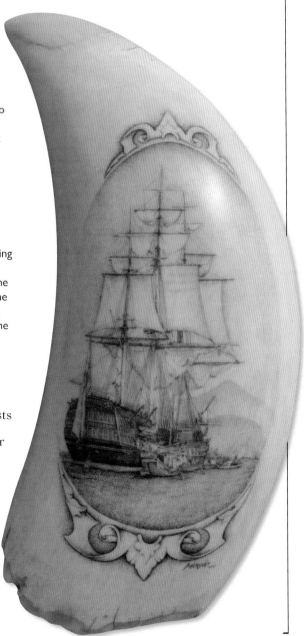

another theory about developing style. When artists
are building skills they must overcome mistakes or
weaknesses. After correcting or improving a skill or
technique, the artist later reintroduces the earlier
idiosyncrasy back into the work. I know that in
a sense there are no mistakes in art, but instead
deviations from the traditions. So what I'm
talking about here is an artist who understands
the rules and purposely breaks those rules.

FIGURE 2.17. **Razors.** This seven-day set of straight razors features the owner's favorite actresses of the silver screen. A few were my favorites, too. Photo by Bob Hergert

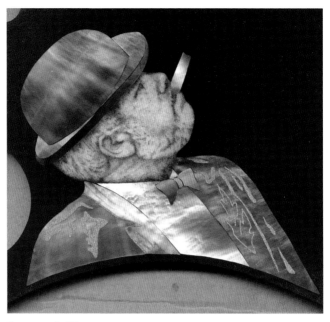

FIGURE 2.18. Larry Robinson did the inlay on this Petillo guitar pickguard. The face and hair are fossil ivory that I scrimshawed. I catch myself being surprised sometimes by the success of a project. This was one that when I look at it I think, "Wow, that turned out great!" Now, if I could feel that way about everything I do . . . Photo by Bob Hergert

What do we add to originality and style to call a work a piece of art—excellence of execution? Certainly. With these three elements art can serve its purpose. It can make us feel. It will stir emotions. It will make us want to return to it. Art tells us something about ourselves and opens up new worlds. It will serve as both a mirror and a window.

3
DAVID J. MARKS

The line between art and craft is not as clear as it once was. Craft traditionally has been considered to be items that are functional and useful in the home, while art has been about ideas that tell a story.

In ancient times, art was used as a form of communication. There is evidence that drawings existed before written communication. This concept is demonstrated by cave and rock paintings that have been dated back thirty to forty thousand years. Drawing is universally recognized as a method of self-expression, and we have all heard the maxim "One picture is worth a thousand words," which further illustrates the powerful impact of the visual arts as an important form of communication.

The American Craft Museum, where I lectured with Wendell Castle in 2000, was originally named "The Museum of Contemporary Craft" in 1956. In 2002, they changed their name to "The Museum of Arts and Design." I see this as a a powerful statement of

FIGURE 3.1. **Long Neck Japanese Maple Leaf Vessel. 2016, curly koa with mother-of-pearl inlaid in the neck of the vessel. The base is poplar joined to the koa with a box joint, gilded with silver leaf, and a 22k-gold Japanese maple leaf design. Patina finish.** Photo by Don Russel

FIGURE 3.2. **The Alchemist's Vessel. 2009, spalted maple burl, silver leaf with patina finish and 22k-gold-leaf-inlaid Japanese maple leaves, 20" high on stand x 7" diameter.** I wanted this piece to reflect a sense of time, mystery, and magic. I titled it *The Alchemist's Vessel* in reference to the process of transformation that we are all capable of when we look inside ourselves and decide to change ourselves through conscious work.

The form or shape of a piece is one of the most important elements of woodturning. With hollow vessels, I often find myself wanting to create a smaller foot, which I feel enhances the overall form. The challenge is getting a tall hollow vessel to stand up on a small-diameter foot. My solution was to make a stand comprising three legs of tapered bentwood laminations. Photo by Don Russel

perception going from Crafts to Art.

Wendell has been one of my greatest mentors and sources of inspiration since I first read about his work in books and magazines in the 1970s and attended one of his lectures at the Oakland Museum in the early 1980s. He is recognized as having been one of the leaders in establishing the studio furniture movement to get furniture recognized as an art form.

Consider for a moment the debates about art versus craft, then try to imagine the complexity of discussions of why furniture, which has always been considered functional and thereby craft, should now be welcomed into museums and recognized

FIGURE 3.3. **Buckeye Burl Vessel.** 2008, snakewood, ebony, poplar, silver gilding, 14"H x 6-1/2"D. The colors and swirling figure in this piece of buckeye burl motivated me to create this hollow vessel. I spent a lot of time sketching out the form and trying to create an urn shape that was somehow classic but unfamiliar at the same time. I strive to make the walls of my hollow vessels thin relative to the piece, and this one is about 1/8" thick. Since buckeye burl is not a dense hardwood, the completed vessel is very light. Photo by Don Russel

as art. The studio furniture movement centered on the idea that pieces designed and built by individuals (as opposed to factories) were the expression of an individual and his or her artistic sensibilities. A factory, on the other hand, may employ a designer, and then materials are coordinated and processed by skilled craftspeople to manufacture profitable items. When a single person creates something by hand, the outcome can create a powerful response in people. There is a connection between the maker and the material that can lead to amazing works of art.

Of course, craft as well as art must begin with a knowledge of materials and their properties, and then one must develop the necessary skills to actualize the vision or ideas

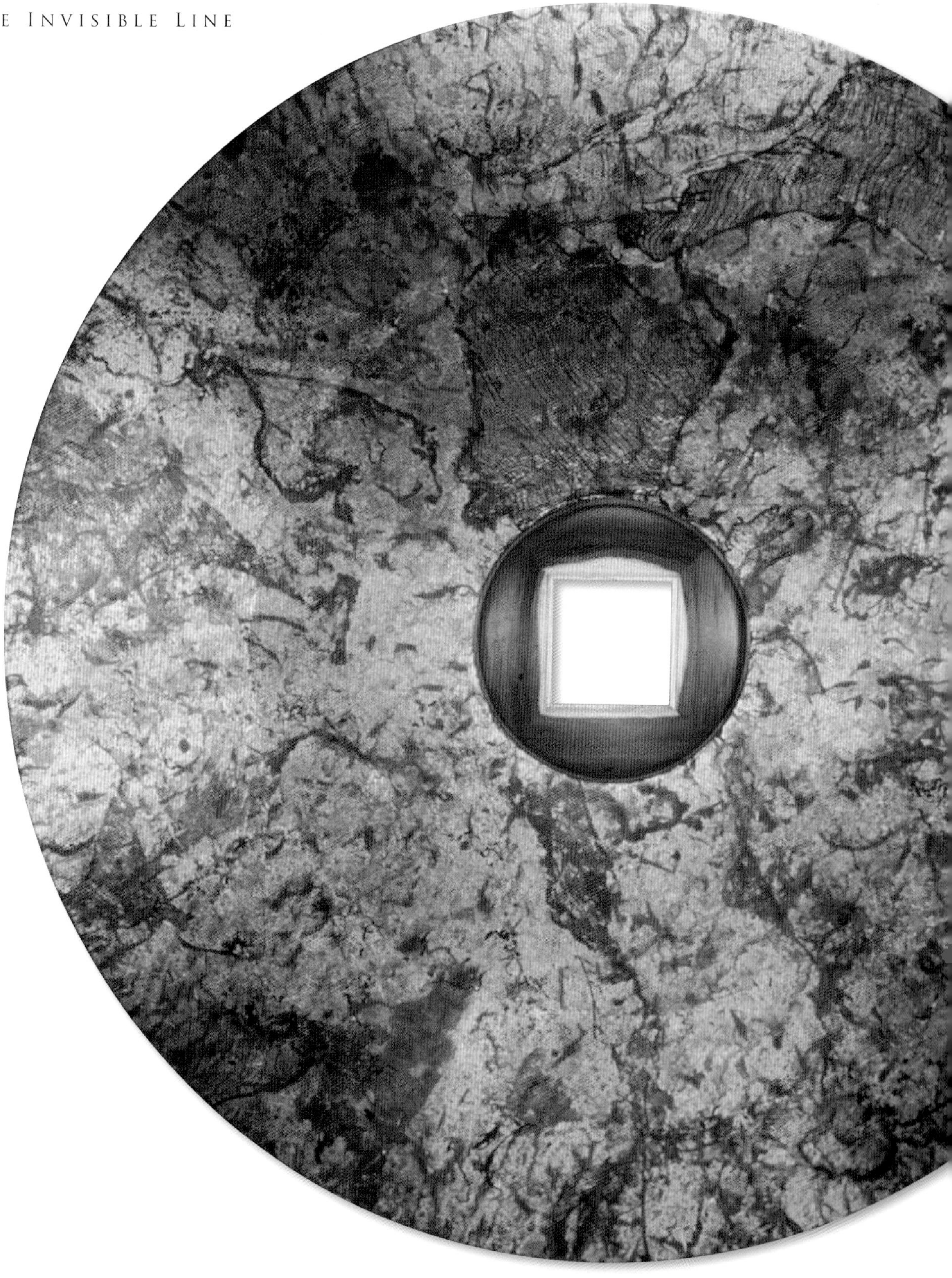

FIGURE 3.4. **Ching. 2009, wall sculpture Pernambuco, poplar, copper leaf & patina, 46" x 6".** The inspiration for this large wall sculpture came from ancient Chinese coins. Round metal coins with square holes in the center were first introduced in China around 350 BC. Something about nothing in the center intrigued me. There is a Taoist message in there.

The large surface area of this almost 4' diameter disc is copper leaf with a patina that really gives it a sense of flowing outward from the center. I created a box with a circular frame of pernambuco wood from Brazil to accentuate the center.

This piece was selected as a 2001 Niche Award Winner in the category of Mixed Media and Miscellaneous Media. Niche Awards recognize the outstanding creative achievements of American craft artists who produce work for craft galleries and retail stores.
Photo by Don Russel

in one's mind. This is very similar to learning a language. The more skilled one is with a language, the better one is able to communicate one's thoughts and ideas. Art and craft are very similar in this respect. One has to spend the years that it takes to learn the skills in order to convey one's ideas successfully. Craftsmanship is about developing skills and refining them, and I am of the opinion that fine craftsmanship by itself should be held in very high regard.

There are pieces of work that you instantly recognize as containing more than meets the eye. We are all too familiar with the expression "thinking outside the box." I would interpret that expression to mean combining things that we might be familiar

FIGURE 3.5. **Time Is Relative. 2008, pernambuco, poplar, silver leaf, Dutch metal leaf and copper with patina, 35" in diameter x 3.5" deep.** Many years ago, an art agent who was looking for a piece for the World Bank in Maryland contacted me. We discussed the parameters and he wanted something similar to a previous piece I had made, titled *Time*. I was allowed to be creative and really enjoyed adding multiple layers of color in the form of base coats of japan paints, silver leaf, composition gold leaf, various chemicals for patinas, wash coats of dyes and mica powders, all buried under and in between many, many layers of water-clear lacquer. The centerpiece is a copper disc finished in a cold patina and waxed. The wood arm is pernambuco from Brazil that was cut, fit, glued, and turned to symbolize an arm on the clock face of the universe. Photo by Don Russel

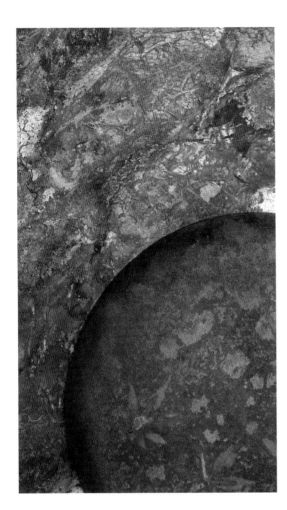

with in new and unfamiliar ways. Hard materials such as wood, ivory, and metal are subject to the laws of physics, just like everything else, and respond to some techniques in unusual ways. So what happens when the ingredients of fine craftsmanship are mixed with curiosity, time, a fully equipped shop/studio, availability of exotic materials, a skilled individual with a variety of power and hand tools, and a mind willing to pursue challenges? The finished piece could end up in art shows and win awards. I began my career doing craft work, and over the past forty-two years I have gradually earned the title of artist working in wood.

Here's a look into my story about how that occurred.

FIGURE 3.6. **Gold Fusion. Lathe-turned, quilted maple center, gold gilding, 37" in diameter by 7" deep.**
This piece has four different types of gold leaf on the surface: 22k gold; 23.75k gold, which is used for exterior gilding; Thai gold leaf; and Moon Gold, which is 21k mixed with an alloy that gives it a silvery color. The back of the piece is completely finished with a chemical patina and sealed with lacquer. The centerpiece on the front is a highly figured piece of big-leaf quilted maple, which I oriented in a diamond pattern in the center of the sculpture and cut into a four-faceted surface pattern. The centerpiece and the sculpture were then turned on the lathe and two layers of gold leaf were fixed on the surface. I wanted to create a textured surface and achieved this by building up multiple layers of a gesso-like putty to make it look more like cast gold. There is also a very subtle geometric pattern hand-scribed into the surface signifying the four seasons, the twelve hours on a clock face, and the seven days of the week. Photo by Don Russel

FIGURE 3.7. **Trilobyte. 2000, curly maple, poplar, silver leaf, and sheet copper with chemical patina, 54"H x 37"W x 8"D.** The title is inspired by the ancient fossils of five hundred million years ago. I designed this 54" tall wall sculpture to be made in three separate curved shaped torsion boxes held together with steel rods connecting them. The torsion box construction ensures that the sculpture isn't too heavy to hang on the wall. This piece weighed about forty pounds. Photo by Don Russel

I studied art and did craft work in my early years of school. Drawing, painting, and working with clay were some of the many things that I was exposed to. It wasn't until I moved to California from New Jersey in 1971 that my eyes were further opened to what I perceived to be original artwork as opposed to traditional artwork. That first year in California was quite expansive for me. I enrolled at the Cabrillo Junior College in Santa Cruz and studied drawing and painting in art classes that I took during the day, while washing dishes at a restaurant at night.

In those days I was searching for a lifestyle, and becoming a full-time woodworker seemed to be a perfect fit. I loved being my own boss and working long hours at something

I truly felt great about. Nature and the beauty of wood inspired me.

I began my woodworking career around 1972 as a carpenter working with rustic recycled barn wood. A friend of mine took me to visit a burl table maker. Upon visiting this craftsman I was introduced to some of the most magnificent wood, with swirling grain patterns and delicate lace burl, that I had ever seen. That's when my love affair with the raw material of wood really began.

I decided that I was much more suited to making small craft items than to doing larger-scale framing and building of fences. I worked in various cabinet shops and spent a year as a finisher for a Swiss furniture maker. Those years of experience led me into

FIGURE 3.8. **Egyptian table.** 1991,
mahogany, gold leaf, lapis lazuli, ivory,
ebony, 71" x 18" x 16". After visiting the
Treasures of Tutankhamun display at the de
Young Museum in San Francisco in 1979, I
became mesmerized by the work of these
ancient artisans. This table is my magnum
opus. There are over eight hundred hours
of labor in this piece. It won best of show in
the Artistry in Wood Show at the Sonoma
County Museum in 1991. The top is a bandsawn veneer cut from quilted mahogany, and
the sides are bent laminated mahogany. Weeks
were spent hand-carving the surrealistic duck
heads, and the eyes are inlaid with ebony
and fossilized walrus tusk ivory. Rings and
crossbars are double-gilded with 23k gold leaf.
Lapis lazuli is set into the ends of the gold-leaf
bars. The braces that connect the duck heads
are gilded with copper leaf and treated with a
chemical patina. Photo by Don Russel

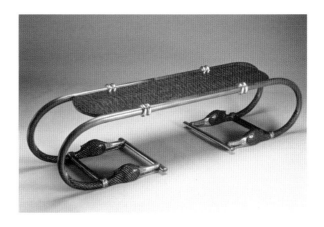

FIGURE 3.9. **Scarab chair.** This is my favorite chair design, and I believe it to be the best one I have come up with so far. The seat is sculpted and slightly lower towards the back. I like the three-legged design since it always sits level. The back is a tapered bentwood lamination that curves in at the seat joint for lower lumbar support and continues down to the floor.

Fashioning the compound curving arms was one of the most difficult aspects of making the chair. Emphasizing the fact that it is a bentwood lamination, I used contrasting pieces of wood; wenge and maple, each in 1/16" thick layers. I had to design and build three different forms before it was right.

On the back is my own version of a scarab beetle, the Egyptian symbol for regeneration. I cut the eleven individual pieces of the beetle from walrus tusk ivory and inlaid them into the back so it would also be raised, and carved it to give it more definition. Photo by Don Russel

doing antique restoration, which was more profitable, and I gained a huge amount of experience and knowledge of wood finishing. I focused my business on antique restoration while gradually building furniture and craft items of my own designs.

Eventually my wife, Victoria, and I were able to purchase an acre of land that had a house and barn on it. I liked the lifestyle of working by myself, isolated from the rest of the world, on our little piece of land in Northern California.

I had a good foundation of skills in woodworking, or so I thought. That same year, James Krenov opened his school at the College of the Redwoods a couple of hours north of my shop. After making trips up there to sit in on lectures and see the students work, I

FIGURE 3.10. **Bronze bench.** 1999, cast bronze with patina, 21"H x 26"L x 11"D. I had made a series of wooden benches back in the late 1980s using this shape and proportions while mixing different woods. One of them was on display at an art exhibit in New York. After the show a leg was broken during the return shipping. This experience led me to investigate casting things in bronze, which evolved into this new bronze limited edition. I made eight of these over the years, hiring several foundries to cast and weld them, and then did all of the finishing and patina work in my own studio. Selected as a 2001 Niche Award Winner in the category of Garden Art/Sculpture. Photo by Don Russel

realized that I needed to learn a great deal more about the fine points of woodworking.

In the early 1980s I was also told about an exhibition of woodworking artists at the Oakland Museum. Art Espenet Carpenter and Gary Knox Bennett were two of the many artists exhibiting there. It turned out they were offering classes at their studios the following year and I was able to begin studying with each of them.

As the years of being a struggling full-time woodworker went by, I continued to

FIGURE 3.11. **Coopered glass dining table. 1987, 6' L with ¾" elliptical glass top. I've always admired furniture with curved forms. Squares and rectangles become predictable and seem generally unnatural, so for this table I used about ten different fixtures to facilitate the construction of a curvilinear design. It involves two coopered columns angled in towards each other and connected with two stretchers that are joined with mortise and tenons. It is a knock-down design that allows the tenons to be tapped out to release the stretchers. The top is glass and has a continuous strip lamination around it. The fixtures that I used are specifically designed for handling difficult construction of curved work.** Photo by Don Russel

hone my skills. In the beginning, my intent was to be able to support my family as a self-employed craftsman. People liked my work, and in the early 1980s I started exhibiting my work in galleries and winning awards. In order to sell my work, I began getting involved with woodworking shows, craft shows, and other exhibits where I could gain exposure to the public. I think it is important to emphasize that I live in Santa Rosa, California, which is about an hour's drive north of San Francisco. During the 1980s

FIGURE 3.12. **Inlaid dining table. 1994, quilted maple, ebony, wenge, 31"H x 48"W x 72"L to 108"L.** This was a commissioned piece. I submitted drawings and was successful at getting the bid. My thought was to use ebony inlaid into the bandsawn veneered quilted maple background to signify branches in winter after all the leaves had fallen off. Photo by Don Russel

the economy was booming and people on the West Coast seemed to be less concerned with traditional designs and more open to contemporary work. My involvement with the Baulines Craft Guild became a huge influence on my work as I learned more about woodworking techniques that were off the beaten track.

After working long hours and perfecting my skills as a furniture maker, I kept pushing the envelope as much as possible. I created work with curves, involving bent-wood lamination techniques, vacuum-pressed veneer forms, carving and sculpting, inlays and marquetry, gold leaf, and various metals with patinas. I went into woodturning in the 1990s, and it has become the focus of my work today.

FIGURE 3.13. **Dragonfly vessel. 2013, pernambuco top joined to a poplar base with a glued box joint, 12" high x 7" diameter.** I have always liked dragonflies and how they seem to mysteriously hover in the air over water, and decided to make them the focus of this vessel while giving it some Japanese influence. Combining the deep red japan paint for the background with the deep red color of pernambuco for the top worked really well. Many layers of mica powders and dyes in between clear coats of lacquer were applied to achieve the effect. Photo by Joe McDonald

In the late 1980s an artist living nearby introduced me to the process of gilding metal leaf and creating patinas with chemicals. I became so fascinated with this form of expression that, after years of studying it in depth and adding it to all my hollow-vessel and wall sculptures, it has now become my signature. I guess you could say that gilding and patinas has been my personal turning point in getting my work recognized by the art world. While I had recognized that furniture might be accepted by some as art, I had decided it was no longer a battle that I wanted to fight. Yet my hollow vessels decorated with patina finishes were clearly what influenced the American Craft Museum to invite me to lecture as an emerging artist.

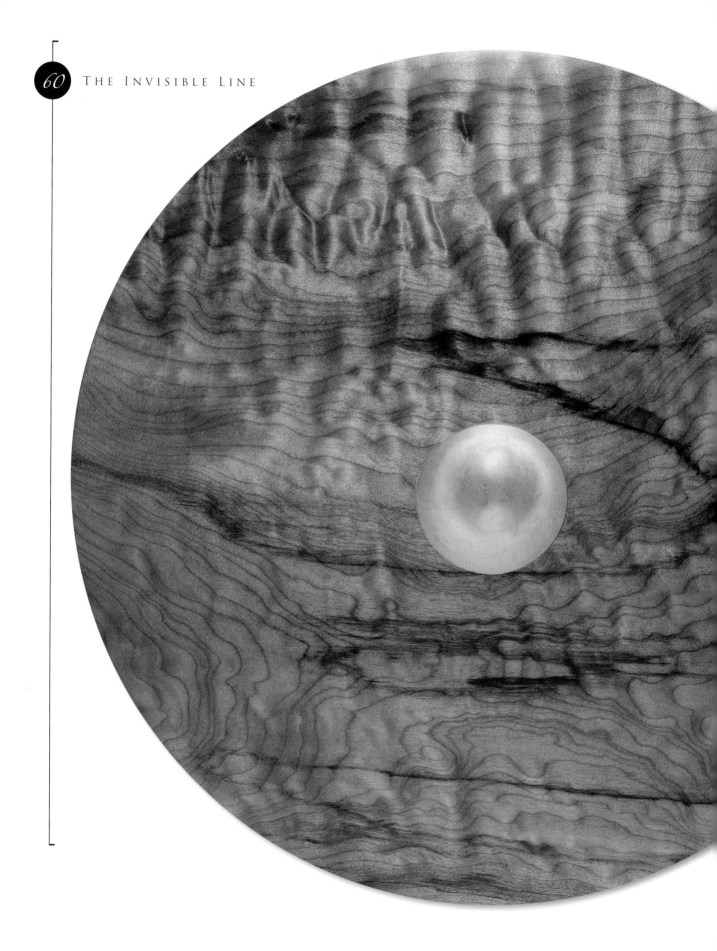

FIGURE 3.14. **August Moon. 15" in diameter by 2.5" deep.** The wall sculpture titled *August Moon* is turned from a truly amazing piece of big-leaf western quilted spalted maple, with the grain illuminated to almost a three-dimensional look with the hand-rubbed oil finish. The center is 23.75k gold leaf. Photo by Joe McDonald

All these experiences were integral in my own personal growth from craftsman to artist. I always feel a little uncomfortable referring to myself as an artist, but so many other people and galleries refer to my work as art that I have learned to simply accept it and say, "Thank you."

FIGURE 3.15. **Koa vessel on stand. 2009, Koa, snakewood, black palm on ebony stand, 19"H (including stand) x 7½"D.** This piece features some magnificent curly koa for the top of the vessel and a segmented rim of snakewood and ebony. The lower portion of the vessel is gilded with copper leaf over a textured surface. A chemical patina creates some darker areas on the copper, casting shadows onto some of the relief areas. On this vessel I decided to go for an amphora shape on the bottom, so the base is completely rounded and therefore needs a stand to hold it up. I decided to use Gabon ebony for the stand because of its rich, classic black color. The stand itself is a major piece of work in that, in order to create strength in the ebony, I segmented three rings and laminated those together with a staggered glue joint. Basically, this is a brick lay technique that creates strength by overlapping the long grain over each joint. After the glueup, I mounted the ring on a series of backup blocks and completely turned the ring on the lathe. The legs are a tapered, bentwood lamination. Photo by Don Russel

FIGURE 3.16. **Tom Cerletti guitar.** Tom Cerletti built this guitar in a collaborative effort with me. It was built in 1999 for guitarist Steve Kimock. The guitar is made of German spruce and rock maple, with a Cuban cedar neck.

The finish I created for the guitar is mostly genuine silver leaf, some copper leaf, and layers of 22k gold leaf, followed with a chemical patina. I wanted the finish on the guitar to be quiet but powerful. Steve likes older, beat-up guitars and didn't want it to be too flashy. The darker blue tones seemed to give the guitar more soul.

Photo by John Youngblood

4
MICHIHIRO MATSUDA

My name is Michihiro Matsuda. I am a guitar maker. I make guitars by hand as best as I can at my highest level of creativity.

But, when I think carefully about what I am doing and the works I make, within the context of art and craft, I don't know how I can categorize myself, and what my works are. I'm not sure why and for what reasons I want to make them. In the final analysis, I can only say, "Because I want to make them whatever they are."

Rather than saying that I can't find words to explain it, there may be no such words that exist from the beginning. What I can do is look at "art" and "craft" objectively from outside of myself,

FIGURES 4.1A, 4.1B, AND 4.1C. I applied the concept of "deconstruction" to guitars. There is a sound board, but no body as a sound box. Any guitar today is already burdened with a representative symbolic image visually, aurally, and conceptually. I am trying to create distance from these symbolic images with this model. It doesn't mean that I try to invent a new instrument, but rather I try to bring the concept of guitars back to the situation before these stereotypical images were developed. The Matsuda #99 in the first image is the fanned-fret version. Photos by Michihiro Matsuda

FIGURE 4.2. **Matsuda M2 #68 non-cutaway, 00 size body (front), and Matsuda M1 #69 cutaway, OM size body (back). The spruce top with a simple one-ring rosette is a fairly popular and common look on flat-top acoustic guitars.** Photo by Michihiro Matsuda

FIGURE 4.3. **Matsuda M1 #28 cutaway. I typically do custom work for the rosette and face of the body, making the rosette differently for each guitar to personalize them.** Photo by Gryphon Stringed Instruments

and then think about their meaning objectively.

When I give some thought to "art" and "craft," it seems to me that "craft" is something skill-based. It has stronger connection to tradition than art. "Craft" may mean skill in itself. Rather, it does not refer to objects that are created. It refers to creative activity that comes from certain experiences makers have had.

John Maeda, who is an artist/computer scientist, said in a *Wired* article, "Art is question, design is solution." That makes sense to me. And I think similar concepts can be applied to art and craft.

"Art" is a question. Therefore "art" doesn't need a subject that leads you toward

FIGURE 4.4.
Close-up shot of the M1 non-cutaway. There is recessed ebony inlay on the top of the body. The major part of this rosette is made of spalted maple and wenge. Photo by Gryphon Stringed Instruments

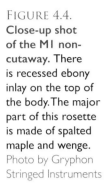

FIGURE 4.5. **Another example of custom work on the face. The main reason why I started this type of fragmented, multilayered face decoration was to add a three-dimensional visual feel to flat-top guitar aesthetics.** Photo by Michihiro Matsuda

something particular. On the other hand, there are always problems to solve or issues to improve in "design." I think there are some similarities between design and craft, namely a centripetal movement that drives them both.

Art can show figures in relationships, and in social structural systems. But there is already something essential existing in "craft" before you start your action, and you are pushing yourself toward reaching something great, but don't have words to explain what it is.

This attitude may be something common, and can't be avoided in skill-based expressions. You have heard the expression "The next one is always the best one." This

FIGURE 4.6. My standard neck heel design. The treble side of the heel has a complex-shaped scoop cut. It is all done by hand. Photo by Michihiro Matsuda

FIGURE 4.7. **Matsuda MI #67 (front) and MI #66 (back).** You can see the side open sound hole on #67. Photo by Gryphon Stringed Instruments

FIGURE 4.8. **Side view of the side open sound hole.** I took the same approach as I do to a face decoration. I like to add three-dimensional elements to guitar design. In this case, instead of just simply having a hole on the guitar side, I applied more complex lines, surface, and space. Photo by Michihiro Matsuda

saying is a good example of this attitude, since craft is driven by this centripetal force. Often this creative expression does not start from zero, but rather emerges under the influence of this centripetal force. For instance, the most primitive material guitarmakers start from is a concept of "guitars." I start my creative process from something that already has shapes and functions. It is not the same as sculptors choosing raw material. Making guitars is not a pure "Question."

This "Question," which is characteristic in art, is becoming important in all types of creative activity, including craft. In this postmodern time, how we recognize value is changing. For example I used to think that there is an ultimate guitar sound. And I

FIGURE 4.9. **Beautiful rosewood back on one of the Matsuda M1 guitars. This custom neck heel design is inspired by a shamisen (Japanese traditional stringed instrument) heel design.** Photo by Michihiro Matsuda

FIGURE 4.10. **Peghead of Matsuda M1 #77. I extended the fragmented rosette idea to other sections of the guitar. Many different wood pieces are included in this composition: a few kinds of rosewood, ebony, maple, and wenge.** Photo by Michihiro Matsuda

thought that finding it and getting close to it was an important value to being successful as a guitar maker. But now I think that no such ultimate "good sound" exists. "Good sound" can only be found in social and historical relationship in the world. Value is not determined absolutely, but fluctuates in relation to other considerations.

FIGURE 4.11.
Experimental project.
I attempted to maximize the vibration area of the sound board by moving the sound hole to the upper edge of the body. Because of the top's honeycomb structure bracing system, I was not able to use the standard bridge pins and designed a new bridge shape for **it.** Photo by Gryphon Stringed Instruments

 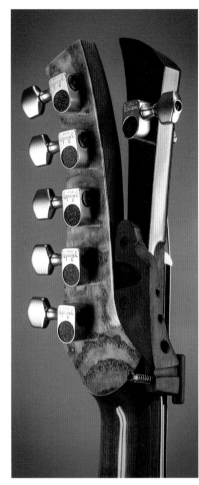

FIGURES 4.12A AND 4.12B. **Peghead design for the fingerboard extension to low D with a built-in capo. The sixth string has an extra two half steps. To make the strings' braking angle even, I split the peghead. One is for the sixth string, and other one is for the rest of the strings.** Photo by Michihiro Matsuda

It would be meaningless to assign an unchanging value to our works. Instead, "the Question" is getting the effective message in our work to captivate people.

Coming back to what I am doing as a guitar maker, "pure question" cannot be created by guitar making, but I still have "the Question" I like to ask through my works. There is a dilemma between "centripetal force" and "pursuing a question."

What I am trying to do is renew that meaning. I am always asking myself how I can add this question to already-existing shape, function, and concept. I think it may be the reason why I am not able to find words to explain what I am doing. It is not genuinely art, but it is also not genuinely craft.

FIGURES 4.13A AND 4.13B. **Crossover flamenco nylon-string guitar. Western red cedar top, cypress sides and back. A contemporary interpretation of the Spanish flamenco guitar for crossover music.** Photo by Michihiro Matsuda

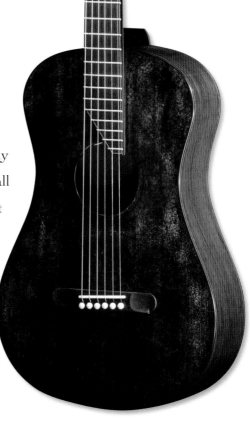

FIGURE 4.14. **Matsuda #85, Parlor-size guitar. This is the smallest body size I use. The face is scorched by gunpowder, an experiment inspired by a Japanese traditional wooden harp called the koto, which typically has a scorched body.** Photo by Michihiro Matsuda

When I create and express myself with my increasing skill and experience, what can I call this? What "Question" can I make with respect to the centripetal force I gravitated toward?

These are not only guitar-making concerns. I can also see people asking more and more "Questions" in many genres of "craft" activities during this contemporary time. With all respect to traditional form

FIGURE 4.15. **Matsuda #106 Parlor.** I made this guitar originally for guitar shows. The yellow, red, and blue inlay materials are reconstituted stones. The black inlay is ebony. This aesthetic motif comes from the Dutch painter Piet Mondrian. Photo by Michihiro Matsuda

FIGURE 4.16. **Close up shot of Matsuda #106 Peghead.** I made the tuner buttons by hand, inspired by the design of the shamisen. Photo by Michihiro Matsuda

craft and tradition, it may be time to classify these "trans-craft" activities differently from "craft."

One more thing I like to note regarding this new way of thinking about craft is that the "Question" in this activity may relate to the total, not a section. From this perspective, craft may not be called something

FIGURE 4.17.
The Matsuda harp guitar experimental prototype. There are nut sliders on wood rails for each of the six sub-bass strings for changing pitch. Photo by Crosswater Media

FIGURE 4.18. **Matsuda electric/acoustic hybrid.** The owner of this guitar was a big fan of Telecasters. I wanted to use a Telecaster-like body outline for him while allowing for originality by disconnecting from the Telecaster as a representative symbol. Photo by Crosswater Media

like evolution, but it may rather be transition. Since the "Question" of a piece can be hidden by its original function, shape, and native centripetal force, the personal information and questions it communicates may be small and limited compared to individual artworks you can see in art museums. But, when you step back, then you see the total. For instance, when you see series of works of a maker, or entire career of a maker, "the Question" may appear in your mind a little more clearly. I think that this tendency is greater in "trans-craft" than in "art."

FIGURE 4.19. This is a ukulele from the beginning of a series that I call *Deconstruction*. There is a sound board, but no sound box in this design. I have made a few ukuleles with this same idea. This Matsuda Uke #90 is a fretless version. Photo by Michihiro Matsuda

5
TOM RIBBECKE

I wrestled with this sacred question for quite a while before finally committing words to paper about what is a very deep subject for me. For most of my young, creative life, I did not take the time to consider where this "line" existed or even if it did. I did not have time to ponder the more subtle aspects of this question while feeding a family and all that is required of an adult life. I am at year forty-three as a luthier and past year fifty as a guitarist/musician. As I write this I expect to carry on well into the future, although the realities of time and remaining runway are now creeping into my thoughts more and more.

A little background about my path may be helpful here. I am sixty-two years old and was born and raised in Brooklyn, New York. I became a musician as a young teenager. I was never the same after playing my first guitar chord at the age of twelve. I grew up watching my brilliant paint-chemist father, Larry Ribbecke, build ship models of extraordinary quality, with plank-on-frame construction. These were from actual

FIGURE 5.1. Laminated "spider bracing" based on the Fibonacci series allows the back of the guitar to act as a more efficient sound radiator. Photo by Tom Ribbecke

FIGURE 5.2. **View through an instrument mold to the backyard of the Healdsburg barn/shop.** Photo by Tom Ribbecke

boat plans. He used the Popsicle sticks of many first cousins and friends. Our family had grown very quickly when my father and his five brothers returned from World War II and began to have children. There were a lot of Popsicle sticks!

This quiet Sunday afternoon activity my father engaged in, while listening to Benny Goodman (Dad was a clarinetist), helped create a belief system in my mind that if you wanted to make something you just did it. Dad was careful to never teach me a thing!

At nineteen and twenty-one respectively, my cousin and I migrated to California together in his '68 orange van to form a rock band and pursue fame. We are still playing together to this day! However, I discovered that a life on the road was not for me, and

FIGURE 5.3. **Interior of Jack Casady's Diana bass shot through the access door. The interior is serenely beautiful. Note the light coming through the graduated top.** Photo by Tom Ribbecke

FIGURE 5.4. **Inside top bracing structure of Diana bass. Bass bar meets X brace!** Photo by Tom Ribbecke

FIGURE 5.5. **Jack Casady plays his Diana bass in a live performance with Jorma Kaukonen.** Photo by Tom Ribbecke

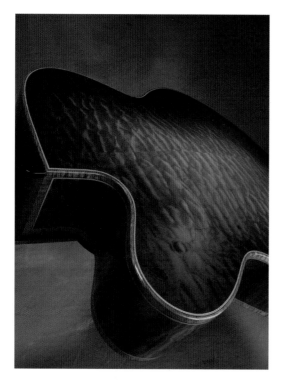

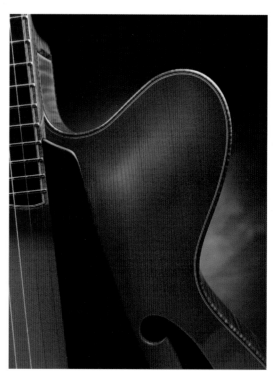

FIGURE 5.6. **Detail of Blue Mingione 11 Halfling™ archtop multicolor refractive blue sunburst in nitrocellulose lacquer.** Photo by John Youngblood

FIGURE 5.7. The art of color is well illustrated here with subtle transition in this detail of the Manzer/Ribbecke Duet. This instrument was a joy to build with Linda. The art of improvisation with two makers! Photo by John Youngblood

that the drugs and alcohol were not the best thing for my temperament. My cousin and I opened a guitar repair store on Twenty-third and Guerrero in San Francisco, just to allow us to scratch out a living. I went to the library and taught myself how to make guitars over a six-month period. This is where my father's example really helped, because I never doubted that I could make anything, even with no training or background in shop. My father came to visit me in San Francisco at an artist co-op called Project One, where I was an artist and resident. He climbed over the backseat of my International truck, still in his East Coast business suit, as the doors were not working well. His message for me that day, after I showed him my guitars, was, "So you're a mechanic." These four words changed

FIGURE 5.8. **Back of myrtle seven-string.** Photo by John Youngblood

FIGURE 5.9. Seven-string guitar in myrtle with inlays inspired by dropping a sheet of paper from my workbench and watching the paper travel to the ground. Photo by John Youngblood

FIGURE 5.10. **Back of Seal's pommele sapele left-handed Halfling™ archtop.** Photo by John Youngblood

FIGURE 5.11. **Detail of Seal's Halfling™ fingerboard and Helmholtz louver. Larry Robinson has inlaid family names in gold in the fretboard.** Photo by John Youngblood

FIGURE 5.12. **Amaryllis inlay from behind the shop, in a seven-string archtop. Airbrushed inlay. This is a recurring signature inlay in some of my special guitars.** Photo by John Youngblood

the direction and intent of my life. What he meant was, "So you have this ability or gift, the guitars are great, but now do something more to change and improve the world with it." In this simple concept resides one of the principles of craft vs. art, what I call "intent."

I have been playing, making, designing, and building guitars for the last forty-three-plus years, and, once past the initial self-indulgence of "Wow! I actually did that," it has always been about creating tools for beauty that will outlive me and somehow contribute to the quality of the human experience. I have always wanted to contribute to the evolution of the guitar. The crafting and fabrication, jig making, and woodworking methodology is the artisan side of me in action. In this sense, I am, in the simplest sense

of the word, a "toolmaker."

I have my process, ritual, and procedure. When I hand my instrument to a player I am no longer the artist, but now the toolmaker, and it is my duty to step back. My hope is that for my time on this wonderfully diverse planet, the story of my life at the finish line will be "Beauty 1, Ugly 0." This is the artist side of me, and the intent is to do more with this than create in a vacuum, and to cause emotional response and movement in the people who are users or admirers of my guitars and my music and body of work.

As I grow older and evolve as an artist, I have seen a clear evolution of intent and emotional power in my own work over four decades. I would never take credit for any

FIGURE 5.13. **End view of the first pin-bridge steel-string private-label guitar. The Halfling™ top shape is very obvious here. Note the flatter bass side of the soundboard.** Photo by John Youngblood

FIGURE 5.14. **In 1994 I used wood from "The Tree," whose rare quilted mahogany is the most sought-after wood for guitars today, to build the last "sound bubble" guitar, a precursor to the Halfling™ style of soundboard carving. A thicker piece of spruce was used on the bass side of the top and carved to a shallow bubble, inside and out, to enhance the response of the lower frequencies. The Halfling tops are just the opposite, where the arch is on the treble side.** Photo by John Youngblood

conscious effort on my part to this end, and have received way more attention than I deserve. It could be the inevitable dropping of testosterone levels as well, allowing me to focus on the deeper levels of meaning, now that I have reached a certain age. I strive to maintain an egoless, Buddhist-inspired relationship with my guitars. I maintain a private practice today in Healdsburg, California, building bespoke instruments in my barn for clients around the world. I call this barn my "cathedral" for my art, as this has a strong element of spiritual power for me.

In any case, when Larry asked me to participate in the book project I was already thinking about all these issues. In many ways my life story has been about evolving

FIGURE 5.15.
Back view of a conventional teardrop guitar in quilted big-leaf maple. A great illustration of the subtle art of color transition and harmony that is so important in the archtop luthier's world. Photo by John Youngblood

FIGURE 5.16.
Conventional teardrop-shaped body with a Larry Robinson inlaid art deco theme. Photo by John Youngblood

from an artisan fascinated by process, to an artist concerned with creating beauty and inspiration in the folks who play and like my guitars, and switching hats whenever it was appropriate.

THE LINE ITSELF

A line by its very definition is a construct, to represent a connection between two or more points in space, and not a real thing, as in a pencil or pen line, or a yellow line dividing opponents. The line I examine here is a border or boundary between two ways of looking at the same thing. It is an imaginary moving target and is always in motion, always changing shape and color. It is important when examining one's own creative impulse and imperative to remember this! This line is not a physical hard boundary but a morphing set of conditions. To the final work in question, composed of elements of art and craft in varied proportion, this does not matter. That work can be a kitchen cabinet, a sailboat, or a fine musical instrument.

I believe that on the deepest quantum levels, the concept of intent can make a huge difference in what the final work will do to the observer or player (who may also, as

FIGURE 5.17. **Fingerboard of a conventional teardrop guitar with detail of musical notation position makers. Inlay by Larry Robinson.** Photo by John Youngblood

in my case, be an instrument maker). If we also look at the definition of what is an artist or what is a craftsman, one of the first things that jumps out at me is that the word "artist" is derived from the Greek *katharsis*, "to purify or cleanse through art." I interpret this in the modern way: to cause growth or change in the emotional state of the observer. One will never perceive a smile the same way after looking at the *Mona Lisa*, or think about joy in quite the same way after experiencing Beethoven's setting of Schiller's "Ode to Joy" or, for that matter, in a more contemporary cultural reference, the opening of "We Won't Get Fooled Again," by the Who. These musical examples were created at the highest level and possess both art and craft in differing proportion, but always cause a

FIGURE 5.18.
Inside of back with woven Sitka spruce spider bracing. Photo by Tom Ribbecke

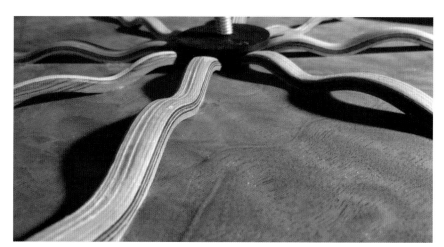

FIGURE 5.19.
Close detail of Fibonacci spider bracing laminate in the Trio steel-string. Photo by Tom Ribbecke

FIGURE 5.20.
Looking through the access door into the Trio steel-string guitar at the Fibonacci-inspired spider bracing. The inside of a guitar is akin to the inside of a sailing ship. Photo by Tom Ribbecke

FIGURE 5.21. This set is known as the Trio and is owned by a private collector. I tried to work in primary colors and coax the shading of the blues and reds in order to establish a smoky, "autumnal" harmony of hue with the natural mahogany and among the three guitars. They feature proprietary refractive lacquer technique to achieve true chatoyance across changing visual angles. Photo by Ray Boyda

reaction or change in the emotional state of the listener.

In my own career there have been periods dominated by both art and craft. The practical tasks of living your life and coping with all you have to do to thrive, survive, and create will dominate for many artists. A kitchen cabinet is a functional instrument (and I love this word!); so is a guitar or a sailing ship, or old wooden cameras. The word "instrument" is by nature, in my view, the definition of something that interacts with its environment to various ends, a vehicle for purpose. An instrument crafted from wood or other traditional materials, whether a guitar or a ship, is still an instrument.

Rather than a dividing line, I see a band connecting "artisan" to "art" across what

FIGURE 5.22. These three backs were precision-sawn from a single 1.8" thick board, by end-flipping and triangulation, and are over 17" wide with no center seam at the lower bout. In this way all three are identical to each other like fingerprints and are all at about 1" depth at the apex of the curve—one of a kind in the world! Photo by Ray Boyda

looks like a giant meter. One side says "art" and the other says "craft," and the needle flows and dances across this spectrum, depending on the intention of the creator, the resulting emotional shift in the observer, and the state of the artist.

I am reminded of a very fine guitar player and student of mine with whom I debated one day about the reason we play for an audience. His contention was he only played for himself, not for anyone else. I was sorry to hear this. My point was that music is communication, and a language, and that when you play to people you are speaking to them and affecting their emotional state—which might give something back to you as well! In this way I believe art is intertwined with storytelling. It should take you somewhere, and if you are lucky you will

FIGURE 5.23. **Hinged finger-joint tailpiece for the Trio archtop with cross-laminate of quilted mahogany and ebony. As the seasons change and wood reacts, the hinge allows the instrument to adjust while maintaining low impedance to musical energy.** Photo by Ray Boyda

FIGURE 5.24. **A time capsule under the fingerboard of "The Trio" steel-string. I have placed all my secrets in this brass and ebony vial. In a few hundred years someone will find this!** Photo by Tom Ribbecke

be rewarded with new ideas and feelings, maybe even some growth.

In my work I pursue all sorts of threads of creativity, running from the innovation and invention of a new finish to the technical enhancement of analog sound. My desire to reach the emotional center of my clients and users requires craft to execute and art to "catharcise"; and, as I am given to saying to my students, "There is no great art without science and no great science without art." I think the same can be said of art vs. craft. I will often design my instruments to appear to have motion or such slight asymmetry that the analytical left brain cannot see the few thousandths' difference in the curvature of the lower bout, but the right brain knows that something interesting is going on! You

FIGURE 5.25. **"The Trio" arch top with refractive lacquer finish.** Photo by Tom Ribbecke

can see this behavior if you have any truly OCD friends. You can move the salt shaker out of place and wait for the discomfort to start. With the use of human perception in the toolbox of the artist, the observer is intrigued and remains engaged and drawn into the experience. The technique of right-brain sensitivity is a tool in the craft box, but to cause the observer to change emotional state or respond is closer to "art."

Some of the tools that have helped artists through the ages to bring forth work that became more than the sum of its parts are classic design concepts such as the golden ratio (1.618 to one, defined by a rectangle's length to width). Leonardo's *Vitruvian Man*'s outstretched fingers, and the ratio of the sides of the rectangle touching his outstretched

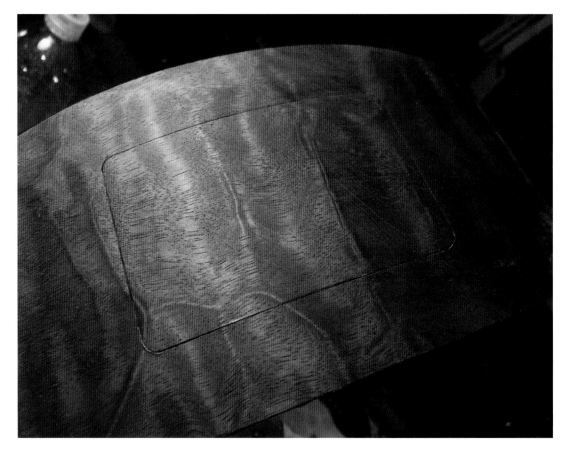

FIGURE 5.26. **Detail of the pierced quilted mahogany access door in the Trio steel-string, allowing almost uninterrupted grain. This mahogany is among the rarest woods in the world.** Photo by Tom Ribbecke

fingertips employs both craft and art to deepen the experience of the observer, and expresses this golden ratio in the universal language of human perception.

The sound of the modern guitar and what is desirable to the player of today is a matter of musical literature and cultural zeitgeist, and in this way instrument makers have always been driven to please and create tools for the artist of the day. Stradivarius in his day lowered the arch of the violin and this created what was described as a sweeter tone. This was the most significant change he made to the violin. I will manipulate the sound of the instrument's natural decay by changes I make in its physical structure (i.e., thickness of plates, dimensions, and the very design of the soundboard itself so the timbre changes as the note resonates and decays), and the results of these changes, empirically studied over many years, will draw the listener in and command interest. I believe that there is no completely scientific way to perfectly predict the effect of an instrument on a particular listener. The instrument maker combines science, art, and intuition in a unique pairing of visual and aural elements to balance visual presentation with the mechanical tonal behavior of a guitar to the end of emotionally moving the listener.

Even in primitive art, although some of the physical technical means were not at the disposal of the artist, intuition about beauty and response to that expression is still very powerful. Some of the most primitive art moves us the most, from cultures where the craft was less important or the artist did not have good tools. In this way the artist uses the tools of his craft to create an experience that will create a reaction, hopefully an elevation of the human condition, although the same principles surface in repression-driven societies, to the end of creation of an improved outcome.

As I try to apply these ideas to my everyday creative life, it becomes imperative to take on projects with the highest goals.

One of the most exciting recent commissions was from the great Jack Casady. Jack, an amazing musical force from his days with the Jefferson Airplane to Hot Tuna today, is still in hot pursuit of "Tone." He came to me after losing his beloved wife Diana after a grueling decade of battling cancer.

He told me he had heard through the grapevine that my instruments had a healing quality, and he challenged me to create a version of what I had patented as the Halfling bass (an instrument with a flat bass side and a carved arched treble side of the soundboard), but to take it to a new level more closely approximating the jazz stand-up bass in a much smaller instrument. This instrument was to be an homage to his wife. He brought me a lock of her hair to include in the instrument's DNA. Jack's hope was to be able to channel her voice and emotion. The power inherent in this project was overwhelming, but I saw its enormous potential. This instrument would have a lifetime

FIGURE 5.27. **Steady hands are called for as Tom carefully fits binding along the curved edge of the end of a fingerboard.** Photo by John Youngblood

of causing heads and ears to turn, inspiring Jack to play to a new level, and hopefully outliving me. This was a project that had all the elements of art, and intent, and also craft, truly an opportunity to practice at the highest level for me. It was also another great opportunity to collaborate with Larry Robinson, and he did the most amazing inlay work on this project. We agreed that this was a historic instrument, and Larry's work speaks for itself. He was able to create inlays representing Jack and Diana's fantasy characters and a spectacular dragon for the fingerboard.

This project causes emotional responses both visually and aurally, and it does not get better than that for a kid from Brooklyn. There is one more element to this project and that is innovation, an opportunity to bring something new to the playing field.

The time finally came for Jack to pick up the Diana bass before he went out on the road. It was three o'clock in the morning the night before his arrival, and completely quiet in the shop but for Mr. T, my ageing cat, who was sleeping in the guitar cradle purring, and my constant companion, a cricket who lives in my shop. But even he was still when I took the lock of Diana's hair out of the box I had kept it in for the last year. It was to go into a special compartment I had made in the tail block, and as I held Diana's hair the sheer emotional power of that moment brought me to my knees. The moment was and is unforgettable, evoking a project I will always remember as being steeped in both elements. Perhaps there is no great art without craft and no great craft without art.

The Bay Area debut of the Diana bass took place at the Fillmore in San Francisco, a standing-only venue. I walked anonymously through the crowd listening as they talked about the new bass Jack was playing and how great it sounded.

This complex moving line, area of intersection, or whatever you might want to call it is the very fabric of our lives as artists and fabricators.

At the end of this chapter I know not much more than when I began to write about my life's pursuit of this thing called art. What I do know is that artistic expression is at the very heart of our humanity and cultural evolution, and that craft serves art and art serves craft, but I am not sure that the line between them is ever that perfectly defined. Perhaps this matter is for the historians and critics. I think my suggestion for my fellow artists is very much what I might advise the tightrope walker, or for that matter the iconic Wile E. Coyote, who lives in a cartoon world within a system of physics with a few special tweaks. I think we, as artists, exist in a similar universe.

6
LARRY ROBINSON

My Webster's Unabridged Dictionary defines "art" as "the quality, production, expression or realm, according to aesthetic principles, of what is beautiful, appealing, or of more than ordinary significance."

That seems pretty straightforward until you realize that it doesn't say who gets to decide what the aesthetic principles are.

"Fine art" isn't much more help—"a visual art considered to have been created primarily for aesthetic purposes and judged for its beauty and meaningfulness, specifically, painting, sculpture, drawing, watercolor, graphics and architecture." You'll notice that the word "inlay" doesn't appear in that definition, nor do some other genres.

Most people tend to think of certain pursuits as crafts, and they lump them somewhere between the strictly functional talents, like carpenters and auto mechanics, and the Chosen Ones, like Bach, Michelangelo, and Picasso. Appearing in that middle

FIGURE 6.1. The body of the "Meet the Beetles" guitar contains iridescent beetles from around the globe, encased in polyester resin. Photo by Larry Robinson

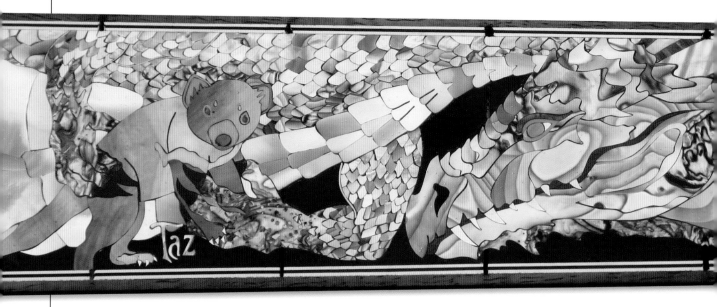

FIGURE 6.2. The dragon and Tasmanian devil on this Ribbecke bass were done as a memorial for Jack Casady's wife, Diana. Pairs of animals inlaid around the instrument had special significance to the couple, and we spent a lot of time going over their physical traits and personalities. All the body scales were hand cut from three species of abalone in the hopes of achieving a subtle gradation of color and tonality. Photo by Larry Robinson

category would be quilters, wood-carvers, pop musicians, most jewelers, glassblowers, engravers, and, yes, even luthiers. Some members of each of these groups can, and have, achieved status that diffuses the boundary between the crafts and art, while many are relegated to making functional objects a little easier to look at, or music that doesn't make your brain work too hard.

Every person you ask will have a different opinion on who should be in those categories.

What are the criteria for placing an object in one category or another?

In my mind, for something to be considered art, it has to have multiple qualities. A

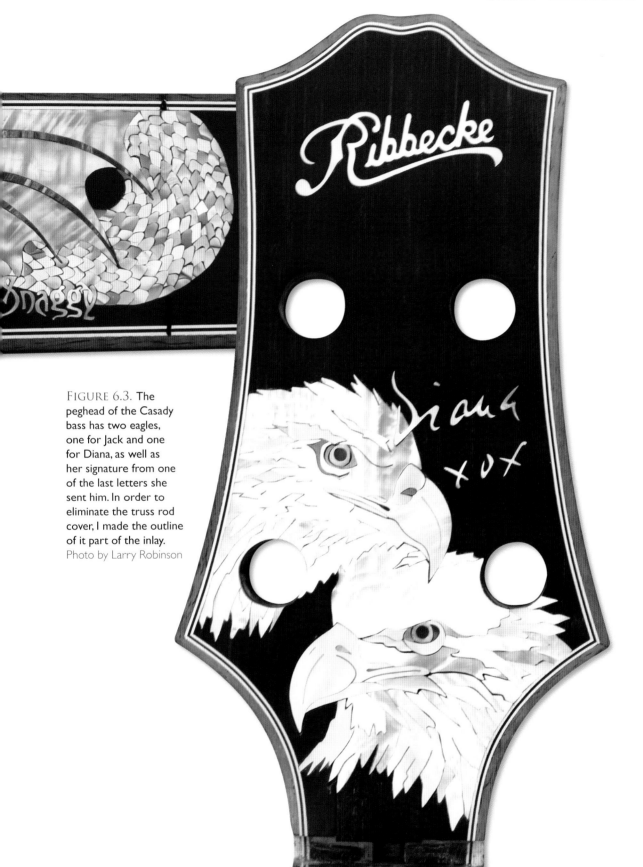

FIGURE 6.3. The peghead of the Casady bass has two eagles, one for Jack and one for Diana, as well as her signature from one of the last letters she sent him. In order to eliminate the truss rod cover, I made the outline of it part of the inlay.
Photo by Larry Robinson

FIGURE 6.4. Geometric shapes are not the easiest things to inlay, but the choice of materials can really make a cityscape, in this case, Chicago, come alive. This one was on a Koentopp Chicagoan guitar.
Photo by Larry Robinson

high degree of technical prowess is necessary in the creation, and the object should draw the viewer into it and be able to "speak" to the observer on several levels. Much of the fine art I've had the pleasure of looking at has left me with a sense of satisfaction and yearning at the same time. An added emotional investment seems to be present in pieces that attract me.

FIGURES 6.5A AND 6.5B. A customer who was fascinated with big cats had me inlay some fairly abstract sections of their faces on several of his guitars. I utilized materials that would make their eyes arrest your attention first. Photo by Larry Robinson

What I do with inlay on a daily basis would be considered (by me, anyway) to be well crafted, but not necessarily in the realm of artwork, although I have customers who may disagree with that assessment. I try to keep the compositions clean and leave enough empty space so that there's tension between what's there and what isn't. The joints between adjacent pieces have to have close tolerances throughout, although

FIGURE 6.6. The front of my China guitar is a collaboration between the inlay of the woman and house, and a traditional Chinese landscape painting by Lampo Leung. All the hardware was custom made and the only electronics are hidden in the tailpiece, with a synthesizer pickup in front of the bridge. Photo by Larry Robinson

variations in line weight are sometimes necessary to give the piece more texture, and the choice of one shell type over another often takes considerable time. The type of guitar, the materials from which it's made, the luthier, and the customer all come into play when I make my choices, but still, there's something else that happens when I manage to make something that I feel is elevated to another level.

Rather than get into a long-winded explanation of what art is or isn't, let's just say that, for me, the process of making something that could last for centuries and be appreciated by generations of people is one reason I'm compelled to pursue this particular muse. That's a key point, the *process*. Many of the artists I've talked to say that what

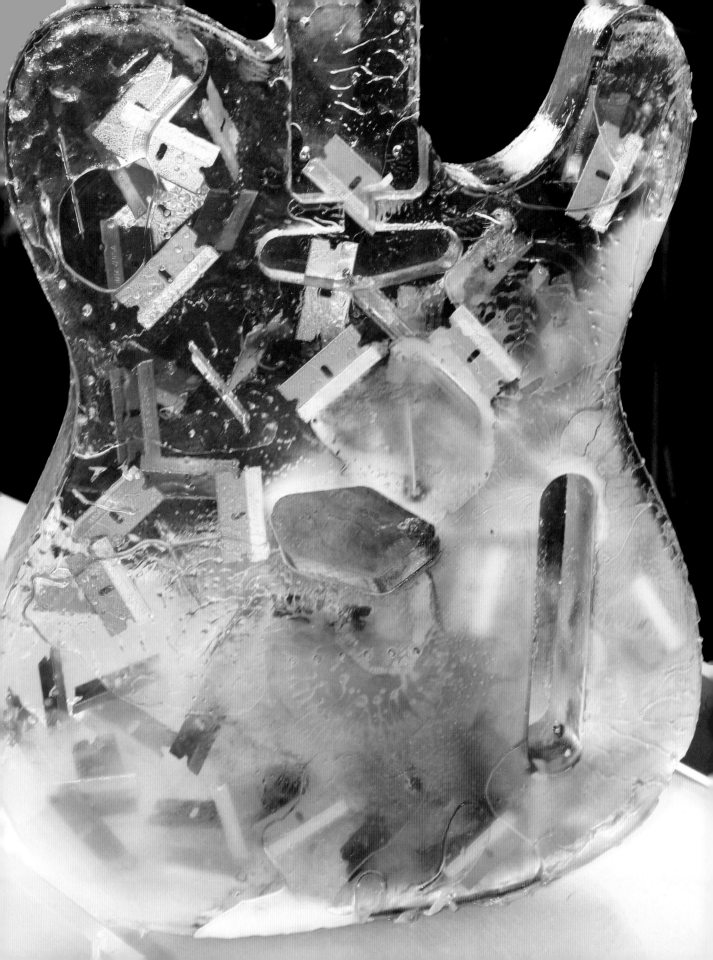

FIGURES 6.7A, 6.7B, AND 6.7C.
Sometimes an idea has to go through many
iterations before becoming a finished work
of art. I made the first polyester resin casting
with the razor blades embedded in it, and the
casting twisted and cracked. The second one
with the colorful beetles in it was almost done
when I dropped it on a concrete floor. The final
one came out fairly close to what I had in mind
(I called it *Meet the Beetles*), and it too was
destroyed when I shipped it to a guitar show.
Art is not eternal. Photo by Larry Robinson

FIGURES 6.8A AND 6.8B. **Here is** a clear example of how the choice of materials affects the overall mood of a piece. One is more subdued, with most of it being composed of shell, and the other has a bold look from deeper-hued materials like reconstituted stone, opal laminates, and dyed stabilized wood, as well as shell and natural wood. Photo by Larry Robinson

drives them to create is the complete involvement and the leaps of intuition mixed with known abilities in making something greater than the sum of its parts. Once the piece is finished, it's a little like letting a grown child out into the world to interact on its own. My emotional investment and technical expertise have gotten it to this point—

FIGURES 6.9A, 6.9B, AND 6.9C. Steve Klein designs beautiful and innovative guitars, and Steve Kauffman worked with him for many years. This guitar, built by Steve Kauffman, was a collaborative effort by the three of us, and featured a Leonardo da Vinci theme for the inlays. My focus for the peghead and fingerboard was to have it look like Leo's workbench, with various inventions, drawings and notes scattered around. The self-portrait on the top of the peghead was expertly scrimshanded by Bob Hergert. On the tail end of the body is a study by Leonardo in three-dimensional geometry, which I accentuated by choosing different shell species for the inner and outer sides of the ball. Photo by Larry Robinson

FIGURE 6.10. The Lindisfarne guitar was a two-and-a-half-year effort of love, inlaying a replica of an illuminated manuscript from the eighth century. The British Library owns the manuscript, and I had to write them for permission to use the images. Kevin Ryan built the instrument using holly for the body and peghead plate, as it looks more like the original vellum than any other wood. I attempted to stay as close to the original colors as possible even though the medium was different. These images are from the Book of Matthew, and my intent was to put myself into the head of Eadfrith, the monk who drew the 257-page manuscript over twenty years or so. Photo by Larry Robinson

now it's your turn to wrest your own meaning from it.

What I like to do with my major works has evolved into a collaborative process with other artists. When I have the urge to commemorate a particular culture or art period, the design process gels somewhat over several months, usually in those early-morning alpha states before I'm completely awake. Then I start thinking about which luthier and what shape guitar would work best with that theme, or if I want to build the instrument myself. I like to collaborate with world-class luthiers, because it's important that the guitar not just be a pretty canvas, but have the qualities it needs to stand on its own as a superior musical instrument. Knowing what I want to do thematically on a guitar gives

FIGURE 6.11. Here is the almost-complete Incipit page of the Book of Matthew, on the unfinished body. In the original artwork there are over two thousand dots surrounding the lettering, so I drilled holes for copper wire and proceeded to glue them in one at a time. Photo by Larry Robinson

luthiers creative license to adjust materials, construction, and finishes in a symbiotic fashion with every artist involved. When the guitar is complete there's a shimmering field of potentiality that surrounds the visual offering, waiting only for a talented player to unlock hidden sonic treasure.

The theme of the artwork also has to compliment (to a degree) the personality of the luthier or company involved. My Santa Cruz 00-sized Nouveau guitar was an homage to the one hundredth anniversary of the art nouveau movement, and I thought it was a perfect fit to have it made by the Santa Cruz Guitar Company, which makes a model reminiscent of the parlor guitars of the early twentieth century. After searching for months to find someone who could paint in the style of the pre-Raphaelite artist John Waterhouse, I hired Michael Coy to paint the scene on the spruce soundboard. David Giulietti engraved the rosette, and Michael Riley cast the emerald-tipped bridge and tail pins.

My Lindisfarne Gospels guitar is particularly suited to appear on one of Kevin Ryan's amazing instruments, reflecting his Anglican Christian roots. The illuminated Incipit page from the book of Matthew was inlaid on the back of a holly body, somewhat resembling the virginal surface of the vellum that the original was drawn on fourteen hundred years ago.

The China guitar (really a MIDI controller, as there are no magnetic pickups on it, just a Roland synth pickup), my first mega project, was completed in 1996 and inspired me to begin collaborating with people outside my range of abilities. I hired Lampo Leong, a Chinese painter, to execute the delicate brush-and-ink landscape on the top of the body, and a jeweler to help with some of the hardware. It became much more interesting to have a multimedia approach to the decorative process, and to incorporate other artists' views into the final edition.

Meet the Beetles, an eclectic electric offering, started its journey to completion as several thin sheets of clear Plexiglas with inlays of fish glued to each layer then sandwiched together for a three-dimensional effect. As the angle of view changed, parts of fish hitherto unseen popped into view. However, I couldn't reconcile what I'd have to do to cover the edges of the sheets with the overall appearance of the guitar, so I decided to make a mold for the body and use polyester resin to cast the fish in place. By the time I was ready to begin, my attention had morphed from the fish idea to utilizing real beetles from around the world. Their coloring and light-refractive qualities are similar to shell,

FIGURE 6.12. A close-up shot of part of a letter gives an idea of the involvement of not only me, but also Eadfrith, working in sunlight or lamplight with a little brush. In my case, the knots were cut one piece at a time so I could clearly show the under- and over-braiding effect. All the dots are in place and 18k gold dust forms some of the border work. Photo by Larry Robinson

and to my knowledge it hadn't been done in a guitar before. There is no wood anywhere in the piece, but it still sounds great.

I like to work a layered effect into the pieces. They should have an attractive and shapely quality from across the room, something that intrigues or captures the attention of a casual glance. As the viewer moves closer, more and more details emerge, and even after

FIGURE 6.13. The copper dots are being glued in place, to be snipped off and sanded when the glue dries. Photo by Larry Robinson

FIGURE 6.14. I felt that some things should reflect the techniques of the original manuscript, so I used watercolor paints in select areas. Photo by Larry Robinson

close inspection over time, there should be little surprises. Letting the materials speak for themselves is important. There is a time to exert your will on your materials and a time to let go. The nacre and chatoyance of shell is ever changing in different angles of light and throughout the day. If each piece is well chosen, it adds an immeasurable beauty and dignity to the overall effect. Natural materials are my first choice in an inlay. I have nothing against

FIGURE 6.15. **From a customer-supplied drawing I inlaid this colorful rendition of a mountain highway in all synthetic materials, like reconstituted stone, colored Plexiglas, and dyed stabilized wood. Only the black road is the ebony of the fingerboard. Original design by Fian Arroyo.** Photo by Larry Robinson

FIGURE 6.16. **Cooperating with your materials and allowing them to have their own voice is an important part of the creative process.** Photo by Larry Robinson

laminates, recon stone, or plastics, and have used them extensively in my work throughout the years. I don't feel compelled to use them just because they're available, but have no hesitation to incorporate them when that's what's needed.

To those who ask, "Well, what does this represent? What story does it tell?" I would say that the answers are different for every pair of eyes that sees the instrument. Dot position markers on

FIGURE 6.17. My homage to the art nouveau period was a two-year project. Once again I decided to collaborate with other artists rather than attempt to do everything myself. I hired Santa Cruz Guitars to make the instrument with my rosewood, and enlisted David Giulietti to engrave the silver rosette, Michael Coy to paint the front of the body, and Michael Reilly to cast the emerald-studded silver bridge pins. I remember collaging various elements to do the back inlay design, and not liking the results until I moved the little flock of birds in the upper left about an eighth of an inch lower. Sometimes just a little tweak can make all the difference. Photo by Larry Robinson

a fingerboard tell a story of a guitar company making instruments as economically as possible. An inlay in an unusual place can tell the story of someone trying to cover up where he or she drilled through the wrong place (been there, done that!). If fine art is supposed to tell a story, then the manual with the pictograms that show you how to set up your new computer might be considered fine art, but Van Gogh's sunflowers wouldn't.

FIGURE 6.18. **The thirty-fifth anniversary of Olson Guitars featured dragonflies and roses.** Photo by Larry Robinson

FIGURE 6.19. **Jim Olson's fourteen hundredth guitar also got the royal treatment with gold filigree cut from sheet, not bent wire.** Photo by Larry Robinson

Sometimes there's no need to have a fixed narrative. Throughout history, tools that transformed society gained special status and were immortalized with highly decorated examples. When I think of this, usually my mind conjures up fetishistic weapons and armor that have become ceremonial and remain unused for their original purpose. Guitars have been a transformative tool in the twentieth century, and, as with their

elaborate counterparts of the eighteenth and nineteenth centuries that were made for royalty, we are seeing many more that have been visually enhanced for the pleasure of their owners. There are plenty of unadorned guitars out there for those who want them for their utility. I will continue to do what I do to them because I am compelled to and

FIGURE 6.20. This Petillo guitar's Sealife fingerboard inlay almost takes over completely, but conveys the idea of a turbulent and lush environment. Photo by Larry Robinson

FIGURE 6.21. I've inlaid quite a few guitars for C. F. Martin and Co., but I think I had the most fun with this one, commemorating the psychedelic era of the late 1960s. Inlays dripped off the fingerboard onto the side of the guitar and then onto the back. Forward and reverse psychedelic fonts merged with iconic imagery of the era. Photo by Larry Robinson

asked to. Anyone who wishes to own one can rest assured that they won't be the only kid on the block who has one. They'll be the only kid in the world who does.

So, returning to the original question, "When does craft become art?" I would say that there's a place for institutional, educated (and overly educated) pronouncements and

FIGURE 6.22. A drawing by Greg Rich had been sitting in my file cabinet for many years before I had the chance to inlay this on a Ribbecke Halfling archtop. Her features were exquisitely rendered by Bob Hergert. Photo by Larry Robinson

definitions on the subject, but there's also your own opinion. At a recent guitar show I had four of my guitars on stands on the table, and the diversity of opinions people offered as they looked them over was interesting. One person claimed, pointing, "Now, *that* one's art!" The others evidently didn't move him in the same way. Some people hated the "Meet the Beetles" guitar and some loved it. Few were neutral about any of them.

In my first year in Sonoma County, California, I lived and worked just down the street from Christo's *Running Fence*, a twenty-six-mile-long, eighteen-foot-high nylon artwork that was present in the landscape for two weeks. At first I thought it was a stunt, but after a while I grew to appreciate it and then to love it, not just because it was

FIGURE 6.23. Occasionally I'll receive a fingerboard that the customer wants to slot for frets after they get it back. In cases like this I think they would look just as good if they were just framed and hung on a wall. This snake was cut mostly from black mother-of-pearl and inlaid into a maple fingerboard.
Photo by Larry Robinson

ubiquitous as I drove around the county and made me really look at the topography with different eyes, but because it forced everyone who saw it to have an opinion. People who had never thought about art or stepped into a museum had conversations with each other about it. Crusty old farmers had to be convinced to let it pass through their land, lawyers had to wrangle over environmental and county laws, hippies and housewives helped put it together and take it down. The real art wasn't just the visible part. It was also the cooperation of disparate groups of humans to let something happen that was greater than the sum of its parts.

In the end, it's up to you.

7
ERVIN SOMOGYI

I've been asked to contribute some thoughts about what art vs. craft means to me. This simple-sounding request is actually a subtle and complex one. Here is my thinking about art and what it signifies for me, in a nutshell, and with a bit of historical context added.

FOR STARTERS, WHERE DID "ART" COME FROM, ANYWAY?

From the time the first caveman had the urge to smear pigment onto a cave wall, art has been . . . well . . . something that only humans seem to do. It is an attempt at representation . . . of things that are both concrete and abstract. As far as we know, no other animal has or needs a representational life. It should be no surprise to anyone that art of any kind is a product of time, place, and culture. On the other hand, the human need to engage in the act of representation is, very much by

FIGURE 7.1. **The Famiglio Project Guitars.** Photo by George Post

FIGURE 7.2. This was a special commission for a client. Lute roses were traditionally hand-carved, as is this one. A lute rose mellows and muffles an instrument's sound, however, and this guitar has a soundport at its bottom that makes it possible for this guitar to sound like a guitar. Photo by George Post

FIGURE 7.3. **Here I'm hand-carving a lute rose with surgical scalpels and small chisels.** Photo by George Post

itself, a deep and surprising mystery.

Whether it is painted, carved, cast, written, or anything else, art is symbolic. It is also, most certainly, the proverbial elephant being felt by the blind men who perceived either a tree, a leaf, a rope, a snake, or a house depending on what part of the beast they were touching. No one seems to know what art really is any more than we know what gravity is, despite the fact that we've lived with both art and gravity for millennia. As far as the latter is concerned, physicists today are butting their heads against the seemingly basic task of comprehending not only what gravity is, but why it should even exist, along with such esoteric questions as why do atoms even have mass? The quest for that

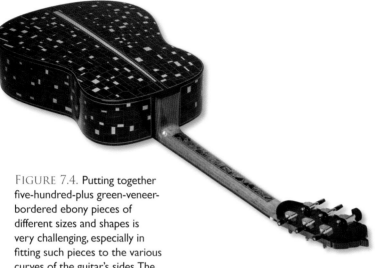

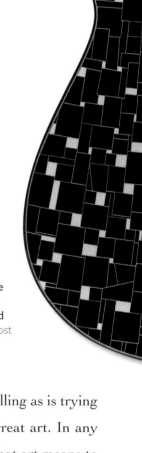

FIGURE 7.4. Putting together five-hundred-plus green-veneer-bordered ebony pieces of different sizes and shapes is very challenging, especially in fitting such pieces to the various curves of the guitar's sides. The design was inspired by the look of some closely fitted-together paving stone work that I saw on a street in a small Mexican town. In the case of this guitar, it seemed to me that the cobbled-together look would be enhanced by adding contrast in the form of randomly inlaid yellowheart wood pieces. Photo by George Post

FIGURE 7.5. **The back of the many-ebony-pieces guitar.** The Latin name for ebony is *diospyros*, and I call this my Diospyros guitar. Not only does it carry the look of the paving-stone work that I mentioned, but it also looks like all the endless flat farmland in the Midwest that one flies over. I love the pattern because it seems organized and random at the same time. Photo by George Post

knowledge is great fun and frustration and, as far as I can tell, as compelling as is trying to understand how a painting of a can of Campbell's tomato soup is great art. In any event, I think this will be a more interesting story if I simply tell you what art means to me personally. But before I do that, I need to give you some general background.

SOME FACTOIDS AND STATISTICS

As far as man-made things go, the U.S. Bureau of Labor Statistics tells us that there are more than twenty thousand different job descriptions of work that a citizen can do, all of which represent some cog in the great economic machine or thread in the great social

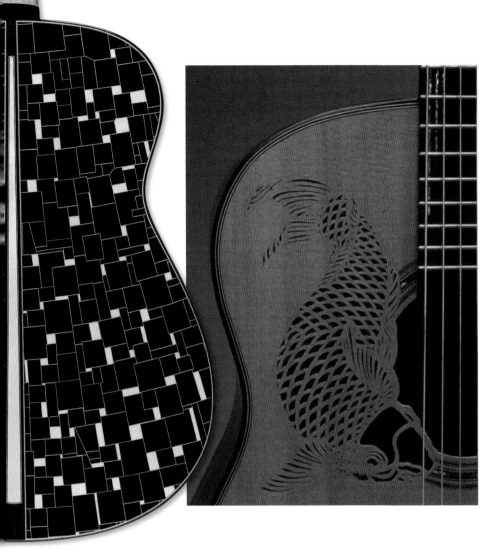

FIGURE 7.6. This is the first ornamental design I ever carved into a guitar top. I had been carving lute roses for years, and at one point it occurred to me that the same techniques and tooling could be used toward a completely different kind of ornamentation while leaving the soundhole open. I like koi and carp fish; they seem beautiful to me. A witty friend quipped that this guitar would be great for playing scales. I had to agree.
Photo by George Post

fabric. Some of these jobs are quite useful in amazingly oddball ways. But how does being an artist fit into this? What, exactly, is one to make of the . . . uh . . . astonishingly useless, personal, and highly impractical act of dabbing paint onto a piece of canvas? Who on earth would ever have started that kind of thing? And what were they thinking at the time? I mean, you can't eat it, wear it, ride it, climb it, grow it, smoke it, have sex with it, or use it to change a flat tire. You just look at it.

Well, as I said, art is an act of representation. It is an effort or effect that carries some kind of significance. Humans seem to have a need to do that. I'm pretty sure that the reason for this is that art gives a particular kind of satisfaction or release. It is

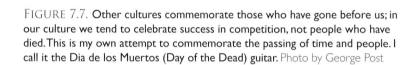

FIGURE 7.7. Other cultures commemorate those who have gone before us; in our culture we tend to celebrate success in competition, not people who have died. This is my own attempt to commemorate the passing of time and people. I call it the Dia de los Muertos (Day of the Dead) guitar. Photo by George Post

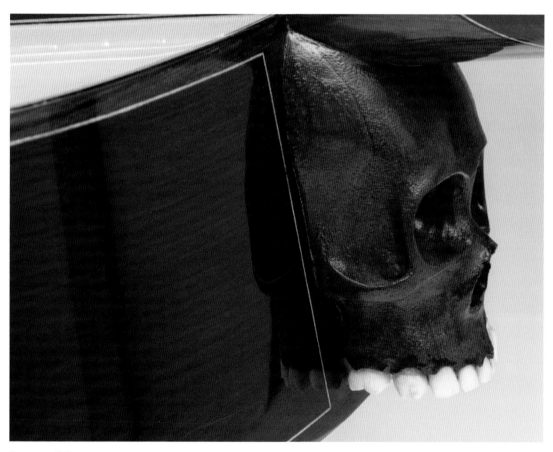

FIGURE 7.8. The Dia de los Muertos guitar has a skull-carved heel block. It is carved from/into the same piece of wood that makes up the head and neck. The teeth are genuine. Besides this being a "theme" guitar, it is a fully functioning instrument with good playability and sound. Photo by George Post

sometimes described, subjectively, as being that which makes sense to you in such a way that you experience a momentary glimpse of a different reality, or feel half-reminded of something that you had long ago forgotten. I think of it as an in-the-moment liberation from tension — as when one has a sense of "Aaah! That's it!" or when one has completed some inner task and thinks, "O.K., I can stop now," and lays the burden down. But that's just me; as an elephant being palpated by blind men, art can really be a hobby, a business, occupational therapy, a practical outlet for creative energies, a political statement, an avocation, a quest for status and power, a personal obsession or depravity, a quest for the transcendent and the sublime, or some combination of these. Art can multitask like you wouldn't believe, and expensive images of Campbell's soup, sunsets on Mars, and the Virgin Mary riding a Harley have been known to fit somewhere, somehow, into this spectrum.

MY OWN APPROACH AND MINDSET

I seem to have an artistic bent. I have always been like this and I cannot account for it; I just accept it as I do the fact that I'm right-handed. Some people explain this by citing brain organization or chemistry. In any event, I am drawn to things, images, designs, and effects that have beauty of a timeless kind, more so than things that seem

FIGURE 7.9. A special commission for a client: a jumbo guitar made from padauk, with almost random ebony-and-green-veneer strips inlaid into the back and sides. Photo by George Post

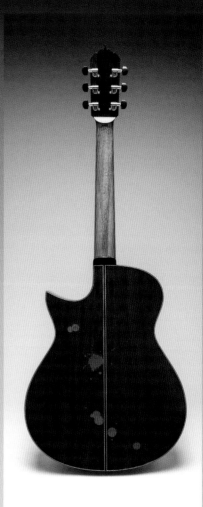

FIGURE 7.10. Trompe l'oeil (something that fools the eye). It looks as though someone carelessly let red paint splatter on this beautiful instrument, thus spoiling it. The "paint" is in fact carefully and intentionally rendered wood inlay. Photo by George Post

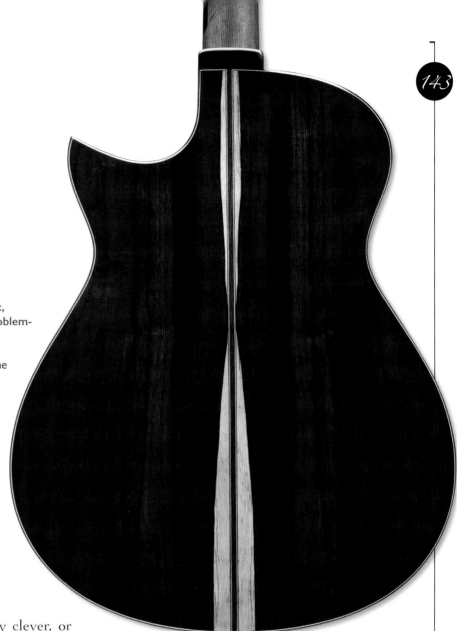

FIGURE 7.11. **A four-piece back, created with a bit of creative problem-solving.** The original matched rosewood back pieces were too small to make this guitar. I added the sapwood in both halves to make the wood just wide enough. The work is seamlessly rendered so that one cannot tell any remedial work was done. Photo by George Post

trendy, fashionable, merely clever, or otherwise temporary. I don't know that I consciously look at things in this way, but I do know that I get more pleasure out of looking at (and making) artistic designs that look and feel "right" and satisfying to look at; and in my case I seem to gravitate toward more abstract and geometric imagery.

I know that "right" and "satisfying" are subjective words, and hence hard to define. But consider that these might actually mean something. The latter, for example, comes from the Latin *satis* + *facere*, meaning "enough done" or "to make full." In other words, it

leaves you not wanting or desiring more. I think good art is art that satisfies, that doesn't leave you unfulfilled by somehow being incomplete or out of balance. It doesn't leave you wanting more . . . or feeling stuffed. Pornography leaves you wanting more, and I'm not just talking about naked people; pretty much any of the glitzy and artistically done ads and commercials with high production values that one sees everywhere nowadays, and whose job it is to persuade you to want one more thing, are pornographic by that standard. Cheap merchandise of all types, as well as artfully delivered sales pitches, always leave one vaguely dissatisfied. Political sloganeering is often disguised as art, and it exists to leave one feeling better or worse than one really is. Calm, balanced

FIGURE 7.12. The four-piece-back guitar is also decorated with some back-of-neck inlays, a little of which one can see in Figure 7.9A. A lot of tropical hardwoods come with sapwood (the white "outer" layer of the tree under the bark). That sapwood is usually trimmed off, because many people don't like the look of it. I do. I think that it enhances a guitar beyond words. Photo by George Post

FIGURE 7.13. **Maple guitar with extensive and exquisite inlay work.** It is easier to inlay things into a dark wood, because miscuts can be relatively easy to hide or disguise. Maple is unforgiving, however: the work must be perfectly executed, as any errors in workmanship will be visible. This guitar was a real challenge. Photo by George Post

equanimity—i.e., satisfaction—is not what any of these is about.

A WORD ABOUT THE BIRTH OF "ART VS. CRAFT"

Today, there exists a division between "art" and "craft" which was, historically, not recognized. To the Greeks art and craft were one and the same, and it was a public phenomenon, not a private one. Art eventually became divided from craft, not because they are actually separate things, but rather because society (and its needs) changed.

That change started with the growth of the middle class and institutions such as the organized church, during the Renaissance—which is often thought of as being a

FIGURE 7.14. Restraint in decoration is an art form in itself. Here, only the sides of this guitar were decorated. I think it's one of my best designs. It's elegant and not too busy. Photo by George Post

FIGURE 7.15. **Guitar peghead with decorative multi-piece top veneer.** Every piece is meticulously fitted into the ones next to it. Time-consuming as this is, this work has no function whatsoever except to look pretty. Photo by George Post

time of art and culture but was equally a time of exploration, conquest, and political and mercantile expansion. As the middle class and the organized church grew in both size and influence, their members found they could afford—and thus learned to desire— private ownership of wealth in the form of land, art, and other things. (The ruling class had always done this, of course, but its numbers were never significant.) In any event, as these new demographics and institutions grew, so did art and craft. Put in plain economic language: as demand grew, so did supply. (We are seeing a similar growth today in China and its trying-mightily-to-be-prosperous neighbors.)

As far as "art vs. craft" goes, this division has been justified by the idea that

craftwork represents artisanal creations that have some practical use or application, while "pure" artwork is more spiritual/creative and eschews the merely practical. In a way, this division encapsulates the polarities around which the middle class and the organized church coalesced: one is concerned with the here-and-now, and the other is concerned with the more abstract and transcendent "after now" . . . at least in theory. In fact, both of these have, like mafiosi, always pursued their temporal territory, power, influence, wealth, and authority very jealously. In a further attempt to justify the separation between art and craft, "fine art" is currently sometimes also defined quite openly as that work which is sold in art galleries. Hmph.

FIGURE 7.16. **Guitar made of perfectly straight-grain wenge wood. It is a good tonewood, but it looked so plain to me that I wanted to add something a bit more visually complex for contrast. Therefore, I inlaid a crosshatch of red veneer strips into the back of the neck. Besides providing visual contrast between "plain" and "busy," I think that the inlay wood picks up the red in the wenge very nicely; this unifies the work visually.** Photo by George Post

FIGURE 7.17. **Close-up view of the crosshatched colored veneer inlay work. Inlaying into a curved and conical surface is tricky enough, but inlaying into the curves at the neck-heel joint is surprisingly difficult.** Photo by George Post

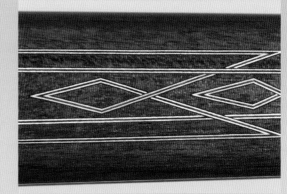

FIGURE 7.18. **A different kind of back-of-neck inlay, this time rendered in black-white-rosewood-white-black purfling strips. The work is all done with Dremels, chisels, and scalpels.** Photo by George Post

Along those lines, some people in that world define art as consisting of paint on canvas or paper, glass, bronze, steel, and marble—but not other materials, such as wood, fabric, leather, aluminum, ceramic, fiberglass, or plastic. I repeat: Hmph.

There is an interesting wrinkle to the private ownership of art, in that it most easily attaches to concrete objects like paintings, statuary, and other collectibles. It's a bit more problematic to "own" intangible and ephemeral art such as music, theatre, dance, poetry/literature, and even some memorable athletic performances; these are harder to possess and keep, and the art must be refreshed at every performance.

In any event, from my point of view, these lines in the sand are artificial and bogus. When art became divided from craft it was at the same time wedded to money, as part of the societal shift that served (1) how citizens of the community claimed identity and/or defined themselves, as well as (2) the commercial needs of the growing art-biz world and its adherents. As to the Greeks of yore, whether or not any of them or their institutions could have taken on the role of being the patrons and owners of privately held art, they appear as a group to have formed their cultural sense of the world, and of themselves, not through possession of goods but through tragic and comic theatre, the Olympic games, and public statuary. While there no doubt existed Greek misers, misanthropes, and idiots (the original meaning of which word was "one who does not participate in community events but rather attends to his affairs by himself") the meaningful culture of the classical Greece was a public and social one. Aside from that, the Greeks didn't have plastic or concrete, and their clothing was practical rather than artistic. They didn't use much wood in their public art because most of their statuary was intended to be situated outdoors, and that material wouldn't have lasted as long as marble does. Those old Greeks may have lacked a fashion industry, but they weren't fools.

(Parenthetically, though, they weren't saints, either. The Greek economy ran largely on owning slaves, which their philosophy and culture—as well as those of all the tribes and nations around them—seemed to accept. I grant the Greeks that they, starting

FIGURE 7.19. **Jumbo model guitar with a hand-carved decorative Celtic panel.** Photo by George Post

FIGURE 7.20. **Close-up of hand-carved Celtic panel.** One can see that it is carved out of the selfsame topwood: the grain lines are continuous and uninterrupted. It's the kind of surface upon which one doesn't want to make a lot of mistakes. Photo by George Post

with Plato, at least, seem to have been the first to question the morality of slavery; still, let's put love of art and truth into a proper wider context here.)

MY TAKE ON THE MATTER

Many of the discussions that take place about art are often beside the point, because this is a territory in which words aren't really useful. What I mean by this is that there's a good chance that if you asked an artist what he was trying to accomplish in this or that work he'd be insulted that he had to explain it to you. Having to use words would be a sort of admission of failure to communicate at a basic level.

I don't think that "art" is something that some "artist" puts into something that he's making, and which makes that object more attractive and spiritual in direct proportion to that artist's talent. In my own case it is more a channeling of something that comes through me but that I don't think is really mine in the sense that I own it as though I'd invented it. Interestingly, the word "invent" comes from the Latin *in* (in, into, or upon) + *venire* (to come—as in Julius Caesar's *veni, vidi, vici*, meaning, "I came, I saw, I conquered"); in other words, to come upon. It does not denote originating or creating anything so much as finding it—as when one does an inventory.

For myself, I don't believe that there's any meaningful difference between "art"

FIGURE 7.21. **A two-guitar project for a client who had experienced a significant transition in his life and wished his very personal story expressed in parable form. The images for the story were arrived at after much discussion, and each of them has symbolic significance for this client.** Photo by George Post

FIGURE 7.22. **Here's a fanned-fret modified dreadnought guitar, with my signature segmented rosette. The fanned fret arrangement serves the needs of musicians who like to play in dropped tunings (in which the bass strings are tuned much lower than normal). This system, in which the bass strings are longer than the treble strings, requires redesign of both the bridge and the peghead.** Photo by George Post

and "craft." I am all right with the idea that, outside of the commercial history of the thing, the *Mona Lisa* was and is a great crafts project. Good created work of any kind is something that has a special personal significance that really can't be measured in pounds, colors, dollars, medium, or inches. And then there's also "art with a capital F," which doesn't measure up regardless of what standard one uses. But I can tell you that good artcraft gives me a specific and subjective kind of endorphin rush.

MY ARTISTIC METAPHYSIC

I make guitars for a living. I work with, and love, wood. I don't know how that came about except that, without having had art training, I spent a lot of time carving, molding, whittling, and glueing things on my own as I grew up—often using this plentiful, malleable, and available material. But there is also, for me, a metaphysical component in my present work. The metaphysic I bring to my work stems, I think, largely from significant losses and dislocations I experienced early in life. I won't go into that other than to mention it; further commentary is outside the scope of this writing.

Perhaps because of those losses and dislocations, however, I can relate to working wood as an act of reclamation and a sacrament. It is, for me, a bringing of things from the past together with things for the future. It is also an act of symbolically bringing dead things to life. I don't believe that you need to have traumatic life experiences to see wood for what it really is, though: it is nothing else than the skeletal remainder of a life form that once lived, took in nutrients, grew, adapted to its conditions, participated in the cycles of the seasons, took in sunlight and converted carbon dioxide into oxygen, produced seed and sap and fruit, interacted with other life forms by giving them food and shelter, held the soil together as it put its roots out, propagated itself, lived a long life, and then died. Actually, was probably killed—just as animals and plants everywhere are killed to serve our species' needs. Every piece of spruce or cedar I've ever made into a guitar top has been some 125 to 400 years old (count the annular rings in your own guitar top)—and that's just in the eight- or ten-inch-wide slice I normally use: the old-growth spruces and cedars are often six feet in diameter! It seems remarkable to me to work with part of a tree that was alive when the philosopher Baruch Benedict Spinoza ground his glass lenses for a living, when William Shakespeare and Wolfgang Amadeus Mozart were expressing their creative genius, when Francisco Pizarro conquered Peru, when Anton van Leeuwenhoek made the first microscope and gave mankind its first awareness of microbial life, or when our great-great-great-great-great-great-great-great grandparents were courting—and which was furthermore almost certainly alive until within our own lifetimes. The phrase about not seeing the forest for the trees comes to mind in this regard, although it's more like not seeing the tree for the wood. I feel that by working with this unique material I'm able to participate in life in a larger, deeper, and more intimate way than by having a regular, ordinary job.

Reality isn't all that simple and linear, though. I have observed that, regardless of what one does for a living, or how extraordinary or fascinating that might be, there comes a point . . . at around the twenty-year mark . . . when it becomes interesting to do something else. In my case also, the excitement of making guitars hit a wall at around my own twenty-year mark; I began to be receptive to doing something new. It was at that point that I got interested in doing artistic woodwork without the need to build a guitar along with it. The result was a body of woodcarvings and inlays that is based in and inspired by the techniques, traditions, and materials of traditional guitar and lute making. In terms of the art-craft divide, this work lacks the practical usefulness of being a guitar, and is more genuinely "art," or at least "really cool decoration." For me, that distinction is not important: I get a thrill from producing both guitars and wood carvings/inlays, either by themselves or in combination. Part of this body of work can be seen on my website, www.esomogyi.com.

In the end, each of us, as adults, carries our early life experiences inside of ourselves until we die. I certainly do. And this internalization has, quite naturally, informed my understanding and expectations of the world. Therefore, as far as the "Ervin as an artist" package goes, I believe that I produce my artwork—whether in guitar or art-for-the-wall form—in part so as to contribute beauty to a world which I see as being sorely lacking in it.

ART/BEAUTY: IN THE EYE OF THE BEHOLDER?

Finally—not that this has anything significant to do with the matter at hand—there is a longstanding academic debate among . . . uh . . . perfectly worthy pedants and polemicists as to whether beauty (which is an alias that art sometimes travels under) lies in the object or the eye of the beholder. It seems to me that this kind of either-or question is of the "have you stopped beating your wife yet?" type; it disallows an answer outside of its own categories. Art and craft, if one wishes to make the distinction, are actually a kind of partnership between object and viewer, which is a concept that I first came across in Robert Pirsig's book *Zen and the Art of Motorcycle Maintenance*, and which I commend to your attention. Also, for anyone interested in knowing more about the ins and outs of the human creative process, I also recommend *The Dynamics of Creation*, an entirely accessible and enlightening book by British psychiatrist Anthony Storr.

AFTERWORD

LARRY ROBINSON

As with most other disciplines that were traditionally practiced by hand, technology has made inroads on the inlay process as well. What used to take days of painstaking sawing and routing can now be accomplished in a fraction of that time. With the advent of the CNC (Computer Numeric Control) revolution as well as giant strides in new materials, we are seeing a manifold increase in decorative inlay work on a daily basis. Like any other alteration in the way we humans do things, there are downsides as well as benefits.

Different materials used for inlaying have flourished in the last twenty years. When I attempted to cut my first inlays, the choices were limited to a few species of abalone and mother of pearl, metals, bone, ivory, and wood. Lately an expanding vocabulary of plastics, reconstituted stone, dyed stabilized wood, laboratory-grown gem laminates, and multiple species of shell laminates have afforded me a surfeit of choices in my inlay palette.

The laminated shell known under the trade name Abalam was patented by Chuck Erikson and Larry Sifel back in 1998. Traditional Asian inlay was done with very thin pieces of shell that had been delaminated by boiling, then cut into shapes and pressed into wet lacquer to form scenes or other designs. When the lacquer dried the artists leveled the surface. Larry and Chuck developed a way to color-match and pattern-match those thin strips of shell and epoxy them together end to end and side to side, forming a thin plate about 9.5" x 5.5". The plates are then epoxied in layers to form whatever thickness is required.

One of the many advantages to using Abalam is that the pattern of the shell doesn't alter much as it's sanded, because the layers below are from the same part of the shells as the rest of the plate. There's always a little serendipity when using the traditional solid plates, because sanding them level produces a different appearance than what was first chosen.

Abalam is a blessing to the CNC operators because the large plate size allows for multiple pieces to be cut before having to stop the milling machine and replace the plate with a new one. A nesting program can fit a large number of similar pieces into the least space possible, which saves a lot of time from changing out small pieces of solid stock that may only accommodate the milling of one or two pieces.

The laminates are also available in many more species than solid plates, partly due to the size and extreme curvature of many species that make thick slabs commercially unviable.

Since computers have infiltrated our world to such a degree, it's only natural that artisans would take advantage of them to help speed up processes that would otherwise have been tediously done by hand. A burgeoning supply of design programs replace hand drafting, and linking them with CNC mills allow for mass production of almost anything.

When it comes to inlays, this has been a blessing and a curse, at least from my perspective. The fact that there are more inlays available in different designs means that more people are aware of them and the infiltration of them into general consciousness is a positive thing. On the other hand, just because something can be done doesn't mean it should be done. There are many CNC and handmade inlays in the world that suffer from too little time spent on the design process.

Over the years I have had many people ask me why handmade inlays usually cost more than CNC-produced inlays, and my wife suggested that I should include this section to answer that question. My good friend Larry Sifel, who inlaid instruments by hand for many years, then went into CNC production, had a conversation with me once about the differences in the approach. He said, "Let's say you have a hand-cut full fingerboard vine that's worth three thousand dollars. If I made just one on my CNC equipment, it would cost thirty thousand dollars, mostly due to programming time and tool setup time. However, if I were to make a hundred of them, all the same, I could get the cost per fingerboard lower than you could do by hand, and certainly have them done faster."

My reply was, "That's why there is no competition between us, Larry. There are many people in the world who want something no one else has, and they want to know that it was made by someone who picked each piece of material personally and that the result was greater than the sum of its parts."

Larry and I were always sending each other photos of inlays we had done that couldn't be made the same way with the other method.

I remember going on a field trip to the UN with my seventh-grade class, and one of the few things that stuck in my mind was something the tour guide said while we were in the Secretariat building. In the lobby there was a large woven carpet from the Middle East, maybe thirty by forty feet, hanging on a wall. The guide told us that somewhere in the carpet there was a single deliberate mistake, because in Islam, only Allah was perfect. Now, lots of cultures have something like this. Some American Indians had what they called the Spirit Bead threaded into a pattern deliberately, for the same purpose. For some reason my little brain rebelled, and I can remember thinking, "How arrogant is that, that you'd feel it necessary to plant a mistake in something, because otherwise it might be perfect?" I've been practicing my work for many years, and although there have been some pieces that I objectively felt were very nice, there's no way any of them were ever close to perfection. I guarantee there's another mistake or two in that carpet somewhere. There are mistakes in everything, things that could be better, closer tolerances, different material choices, and everyone has a differing opinion about what constitutes perfection. As craftspeople and artists we all chase perfection, but, like the frog that jumps half the length of its last jump each time, we never get to the finish line. Once perfection is achieved, where can you go from there? The struggle to do better at each attempt is a component of making art, although it may not be apparent in the finished piece.

As far as CNC work goes, there is less of the human hand involved than the human mind, and although the pieces fit together more closely than can be done manually, there is something sterile and lifeless to me about the lack of variation in line weight between pieces or the fact that each one of a run of fifty pieces will look exactly like another. Also, the need to use the large plates of Abalam to save machining time ensures a tonal sameness

A.1. **Pickguard detail of CF Martin D-100, based on the inlay design of the millionth Martin, and executed by Pearlworks, in Maryland. Fifty of these were made using CNC techniques.** Photo by Larry Robinson

to the pieces, both individually and side by side in the batch. There are no little surprises where a richly textured piece of abalone transitions to smooth pastel shades as would happen with the use of solid plates. Acute interior angles will have a small radius instead of a sharp point, as they would if cut by hand with a jeweler's saw. Looking closely at the edges of the pieces will reveal chatter marks or serrations showing they were cut by hand with a jeweler's saw, or the absolutely smooth lines of a horizontal milling machine. You may think, "What's the difference?" but the eye picks up all sorts of information that

A.2. **Top inlays of CF Martin #1,000,000.** This instrument is covered more in depth in my book, *The Art of Inlay.*
Photo by Larry Robinson

the brain doesn't turn into conscious thought. Personally, I am attracted to the humanity showing through the work as much as I am to the work itself.

This is in no way an indictment of the CNC process, just an observation, admittedly biased, about the differences in each approach.

Here, as an example, are two photos of a section of the C. F. Martin #1,000,000, which I was privileged to inlay, and one of fifty D-100s, which Larry Sifel programmed and executed before he passed away. Beautifully done, my friend.

ACKNOWLEDGMENTS

I'd like to thank my friends and fellow contributors to this book. They all could have authored something like this but were happy to combine their time and expertise for something that will hopefully be greater than the sum of its parts.

No book comes to light without the efforts of a team of people at the publishing house, and for that, thanks to my publisher, John Cerullo; to the book designer, Damien Castaneda; and to project editor Lindsay Wagner and her crew of layout artists, publicity people, typesetters, editors, and proofreaders.

Many people have helped my career path throughout the years. You know who you are. In particular, it's been a pleasure to have Rick Turner and Frank Fuller as friends and cohorts.

And to my wife and daughters: you are the reason I do this.

CONTRIBUTORS

DAVID GIULIETTI

Buying a book in a coffee shop during a post-graduation road trip up the California coast didn't seem like a significant event at the time, but a copy of *The Complete Metalsmith* sowed the seed for a future as a jewelry artist. After growing his skill set working at a bronze foundry, welding together the cast metal pieces of sculptures, David later moved into a job building metal-body guitars for National Resophonic Guitars. There, a coworker sold him two gravers (small hand chisels for engraving metal), and David taught himself how to engrave from a book at home in his spare hours. In very little time he was engraving metal guitar bodies in his garage for National and embellishing objects for other musical instrument makers around the country. Engraving on other people's work was interesting but not entirely satisfying. The little jewelry-making book supplied the answer. David began to make his own jewelry pieces and engrave them. He now works each day in his Berkeley, California, studio to create jewelry pieces of enduring beauty, and still finds time to take on engraving commissions for private clients around the world.

John Mayer, Katy Perry, Dan Auerbach of the Black Keys, Jackson Browne, and David Grisman all have David's work in their collections. He has worked on the Millionth Martin Guitar with world-class inlay artist Larry Robinson and has had his work exhibited at the Museum of Making Music in Carlsbad, California. His

DAVID GIULIETTI. Photo by Larry Robinson

work appeared in the Lark Books publication *Showcase 500 Art Necklaces* in 2013.

David Giulietti Contact Information

Website: www.engraverdavid.com

E-mail Address: david@engraverdavid.com

Phone Number: 510-558-2356

BOB HERGERT. Photo by Bob Hergert

BOB HERGERT

Before he could write, Bob Hergert would draw. By age ten he was drawing elaborate scenes in pen and ink. He pored over how-to books, comics, and a childhood favorite, *Mad* magazine. He drew pictures of model cars he built, copied the works of any illustrator he could find, and let his imagined life take the form of drawings. He drew what he saw, and what he imagined.

Bob started doing scrimshaw in 1978 in the Pacific Northwest, strongly influenced by the Bellingham School in neighboring Washington State. Soon after Bob was introduced to knife maker and author Gary Kelley, Gary had Bob work on his miniature knives. One of these knives made the cover of *Blade* magazine, which drew other makers and collectors into Bob's orbit.

Scrimshaw Connection, by Bob Engnath and Eva Halat's book, *Contemporary Scrimshaw*, feature Hergert's work in both their editions.

A chance meeting with Eric Galletta of Galletta Guitars has opened the door for Bob to do work for the Allman Brothers Band, the Beach Boys, and many other guitarists. He continues to work with other luthiers and inlay artists, including Larry Robinson and Harvey Leach. He collaborated with Harvey on Martin Guitar's 1.5 millionth guitar, "Da Vinci Unplugged," now on display in the Martin Museum, and with Larry on the Steve Klein Da Vinci homage more recently.

Bob has garnered a following of avid collectors but still accepts commissions. His website draws interest worldwide and has led to many interesting contacts, including author Steve Perry, who featured him as a character in two Tom Clancy Net Force novels, *Point of Impact* and *Cybernation*.

Bob lives in a small town on the southern Oregon coast, which he finds conducive for concentrating on the intense precision and detail that scrimshaw demands.

Bob Hergert Contact Information

Websites: www.scrimshander.com

www.bobhergert.com

E-mail Address: hergert@scrimshander.com

Phone Number: 541-332-3010

Mailing Address:

Bob Hergert

12 Geer Circle

Port Orford, OR 97465

DAVID J. MARKS

David J. Marks is recognized internationally as a master craftsman of fine furniture, turner, sculptor, and host of the television show *WoodWorks*. David hosted ninety-one episodes of *WoodWorks*, which debuted on HGTV and the DIY Network

DAVID J. MARKS. Photo by John Youngblood

in 2001. The show won critical acclaim and aired on the DIY Network for six years.

David started woodworking in 1972, making redwood burl tables. In 1981, he opened his own shop/studio and built one-of-a-kind furniture. In the late 1980s he shifted focus to woodturning and sculpture. His signature patina finish is a hybrid of multiple finishes that he has developed. It combines painting, gilding (metal leafing), chemical patinas, and lacquering techniques. The complex layers result in a finish that may look ancient, metallic, or even petrified stone.

David J. Marks Contact Information

Website: www.djmarks.com

Facebook: David J. Marks Woodworking School

E-mail Address: david@djmarks.com

Phone Number: 707-526-6280

Mailing Address:

David J. Marks

2128 Marsh Road

Santa Rosa, CA 95403

MICHIHIRO MATSUDA

Michihiro Matsuda was born in Nogoya and raised in Tokyo, Japan.

Pairing traditional woodworking skills with an innovative sense of design and construction, he builds around eight guitars each year at his shop in Redwood City, California. He strives to make instruments that integrate fine materials with his dedicated sound study. Each of

MICHIHIRO MATSUDA. Photo by Michihiro Matsuda

his guitars is unique, personal, and individual.

His wish is that Matsuda guitars are more than just tools for music, and that his artistic influence will inspire players to even greater creative heights.

Michihiro Matsuda Contact Information

Website: www.matsudaguitars.com

E-mail Address: info@matsudaguitars.com

Phone Number: 650-362-3599

Mailing Address:

Michihiro Matsuda

3049 Hoover Street

Redwood City, CA 94063

TOM RIBBECKE

Tom has been building and designing all types of guitars for over forty years. He has developed an international reputation for building the archtop guitar, for innovating in all areas of lutherie, and most recently for inventing/developing the Halfling™ line of carved-top instruments,

TOM RIBBECKE. Photo by John Youngblood

which hybridize the archtop and steel-string styles.

These instruments are made one at a time to the highest standards on the planet. Tom has taught guitar making for many years and recently has begun to develop the Ribbecke Center for Stringed Instruments, to teach, create, and do research at his Healdsburg barn private shop.

Contrary to rumors, Tom will not be retiring anytime soon!

Tom Ribbecke Contact Information

Website: www.ribbecke.com

E-mail Address: ribguitar@aol.com

Phone Number: 707-888-5072

Mailing Address:

Ribbecke Guitars

PO Box 2215

Healdsburg, CA 95448

LARRY ROBINSON

Larry Robinson has been working with wood since his father showed him how to use tools at age six. Following high school he was apprenticed for three years to a luthier in Connecticut,

LARRY ROBINSON. Photo by Mark Repp

and afterwards he moved to California, where he worked at Alembic Guitars, Turner Guitars, and the Modulus Graphite guitar company. In 1984 Larry decided to be self-employed, specializing in inlay work. Everything from customers' initials to CF Martin & Co.'s one-millionth guitar has been through his shop. Larry teaches inlay classes, wrote *The Art of Inlay*, and produced three DVDs about inlay techniques. He still builds the occasional guitar and plays bass with various musicians in the area.

Larry Robinson Contact Information

Website: www.robinsoninlays.com

Facebook: Robinson Custom Inlays

E-mail Address: larry@robinsoninlays.com

Phone Number: 707-829-2446

Mailing Address:

Larry Robinson

PO Box 308

Valley Ford, CA 94972

ERVIN SOMOGYI

Ervin Somogyi is one of the "grand old pioneers" of American (and increasingly world) lutherie. Having started as a young guitar maker almost fifty years ago, fueled by all the normal energies, focus, and talent that young people

ERVIN SOMOGYI. Photo by Brent Stuntzner

invest in their work, he now sees his influence as a teacher emerging as his most significant long-term contribution. He has lectured extensively, trained a number of the up-and-coming members of the younger lutherie generation, and added to the bibliography of modern lutherie by authoring two textbooks and well over a hundred articles on every aspect of the craft.

Ervin Somogyi Contact Information

Website: www.esomogyi.com

E-mail Address: esomogyi@aol.com

Phone Number: 510-652-5123

Mailing Address:

Ervin Somogyi

516 52nd Street

Oakland, CA 94609